**The Politics and Administration
of Land Use Control**

The Politics and Administration of Land Use Control

The Case of Fairfax County,
Virginia

Terry Spielman Peters

Lexington Books
D.C. Heath and Company
Lexington, Massachusetts
Toronto   London

Library of Congress Cataloging in Publication Data
Peters, Terry Spielman.
   The politics and administration of land use control

   Bibliography: p.
   1. Land—Virginia—Fairfax Co. 2. Zoning—Fairfax Co., Va. I. Title.
HD211.V8P48   309.2'5'09755291   74-16144
ISBN 0-669-96255-4

International Standard Book Number: 0-669-96255-4

Library of Congress Catalog Card Number: 74-16144

Contents

List of Figures

List of Tables

List of Abbreviations

APF   —Adequate Public Facilities
BZA   —Board of Zoning Appeals
CIP   —Capital Improvements Program
DCD   —Department of County Development
DPLUC —Department of Planning and Land Use Control
DPW   —Department of Public Works
EIS   —Environmental Impact Statement
EQAC   —Environmental Quality Advisory Council
NCPC   —National Capital Planning Commission
OCP   —Office of Comprehensive Planning
OEA   —Office of Environmental Affairs
OMB   —Office of Management and Budget
ORS   —Office of Research and Statistics
PC   —Planning Commission
PDC   —Planned Development Commercial
PDH   —Planned Development Housing
PLUS   —Planning and Land Use System
RPC   —Residential Planned Community
TDR   —Transferable Development Rights
UDIS   —Urban Development Information System
ZOSC   —Zoning Ordinance Study Committee

Acknowledgments

I would like to express my appreciation to the faculty members at Virginia Polytechnic Institute and State University who guided me in this work. Professor Joseph L. Intermaggio assisted me in formulating the conceptual framework for the study and in obtaining and organizing materials. Professors Adam W. Herbert and Richard M. Yearwood provided me with a vital background in administrative policymaking and land use regulation.

I also want to thank the officials and citizens, particularly in Fairfax County, who furnished me with information and insights regarding local government and growth control. Their cooperation enabled me to conduct the field research that is the core of this study.

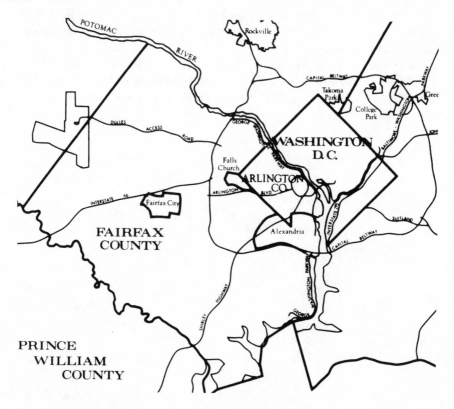

Figure 1. Metropolitan Washington Area. Note: Prepared by The Metropolitan Washington Council of Governments.

Introduction

Overview

Fairfax County, Virginia, is orchestrating its own version of the "quiet revolution" in land use control that is sweeping the nation. On 11 June 1973 the Board of Supervisors adopted a Planning and Land Use System (PLUS), designed to place the initiative for development in public hands. PLUS embodies a reorientation in governmental philosophy and strategy from past planning and land use practices. Previous boards were equivocal about public regulation of growth, and their positions had to be gleaned from an analysis of their actions. In contrast, the present board assumed a definitive stance and established specific policies and programs to accomplish its stated goals.

Notwithstanding, this Planning and Land Use System is also the culmination of gradual transition rather than a radical departure in attitude and approach. Local resistance to suburbanization appeared with the influx of World War II veterans to the Washington, D.C. metropolitan area during the late 1940s.[1] Unlike their predecessors over the past twenty-five years, the current supervisors possess both the political mandate and administrative mechanisms necessary to make a significant impact on the development process.

Public backing and techniques alone cannot guarantee successful implementation of the board's policies and programs. The county's governing body operates within an institutional framework that encompasses national, state, and regional, as well as local, factors. These factors vary in their area of influence, the extent of control that the board exercises over them, and the type of impact that they might have on the adopted Planning and Land Use System. For example, a factor at the state level might consist of legislation that is subject to limited interpretation by the board and that reinforces the board's policies. To ensure the implementation of its policies, the governing body must recognize all factors that impinge on local regulation of growth and must make appropriate responses to each.

The board's present perspective precludes adequate consideration of all critical influences on its decisions about development controls. This outlook creates conceptual and functional incongruence between its actions and the larger context that threatens the future of its strategy. The board has approved piecemeal modifications in the structure and operation of some agencies currently involved in the policy implementation process. But it has failed to develop a comprehensive administrative component for its growth management program. A broad approach that takes account of intervening variables external to county government and that anticipates administrative ramifications of new policies is essential to ensure acceptance of PLUS and to promote coordination of local governmental activities.

In addition, the fundamental shift from private to public management of growth proposed in PLUS requires time to transpire. Yet the board has excessively telescoped the transition period. For a variety of political and administrative reasons, the original completion date set for program development is mid-1975. Considering the range of planning and other regulatory components contained in PLUS, this timetable makes adequate adjustment by public officials, developers, and citizens difficult. Compressing the interim stage between pre-existing and anticipated land use controls magnifies the importance of a comprehensive orientation.

The purpose of this research is to devise both a conceptual framework and an administrative program for effective implementation of the Fairfax County Supervisors' Planning and Land Use System. To accomplish this dual objective, the study is organized into the following two parts: (1) background trends affecting the climate for land use control in Fairfax County, and (2) public management of growth in Fairfax County.

The first part deals with local, regional, state, and national factors that have promoted or stymied public activism in land use control. Recent trends in county suburbanization, expanded planning and land use regulation by other governments, local politics and administration, and county planning and land use control are explored.

The resulting profile of the residents and government of Fairfax County and the forces that shaped their development will serve as the basis for evaluating the board's capacity for achieving its stated goals. This background study is particularly important because many of its elements continue to influence the board's commitment to limit growth.

The second part addresses current public activities relating to land use control. To provide a frame of reference for analyzing county planning and development regulation, general governmental politics involving the elected Board of Supervisors, career bureaucracy, and appointed advisory bodies are examined. Then the board's initial growth control measures and the present Planning and Land Use System are analyzed.

The appraisal of PLUS focuses on legitimization, policymaking, program development, and implementation. The county government has undertaken the first three stages, and recommendations for improving its efforts are made. Implementation has been largely sidestepped as an overt and open public process. Therefore original proposals for long and short-range administration of PLUS are presented.

Since PLUS is currently unfolding, much of the analysis deals with proposed rather than actual operations. However, current events prove that many potential problems have in fact arisen, and they substantiate the approach that the timing of PLUS demands. Furthermore, the basic thrust of the assessment is amelioration of PLUS. Major modifications in the substance and conduct of the endeavor are suggested. Therefore, disparities between original local plans and real activities do not invalidate the proposals developed in this study.

Part I: Background Trends Affecting the Climate for Planning and Land Use Control in Fairfax County

Introduction to Part I

In adopting the Planning and Land Use System (PLUS), the Fairfax County supervisors fulfilled a campaign pledge that a majority of the voters had supported. The 1971 and 1972 election results indicated popular demand for stronger growth controls, and the 1973 enactment of PLUS increased official capacity to regulate development. This demand and capacity are local products of a continuing political process that has spanned more than a decade and encompassed government, the private sector, and the general public.

Since the early 1960s, public regulation of private development nationally has expanded at all levels of government. While localities gained additional authority, they lost the exclusive rights to land use control that they previously enjoyed. Despite this erosion of their monopoly, local governments remain the vanguard of the "quiet revolution," because pressure for development still originates at the local level. To evaluate the offensive that the Board of Supervisors has launched, it is necessary to determine the limits of local leadership in land use control. These limits derive from the political context within which the county governing body operates.

The political arena of the board includes diverse levels of government: federal, state, regional (specifically the Metropolitan Washington Council of Governments), and local, both in Fairfax County and other jurisdictions. Non-governmental levels include: the residents of Fairfax County and the general public, the local housing industry, and the national mortgage market. Although the voters and supervisors chose the county's orientation toward land use regulation, all of the above actors played a part in this local decision. Political, economic, and philosophical contributions that these participants have made since the 1960s most strongly influence the impetus for local growth control.

As one objective of this analysis is to determine the limits of local leadership as a basis for evaluating the PLUS program, no attempt will be made to catalog all groups in the political arena and their exact impact. Rather, dominant participants and their major contributions, as illustrated by recent trends in Fairfax County, will be emphasized. This selective approach is justified on the grounds that the analysis is concerned as much with the dynamics of decision making in this political arena as with its results.

There are three reasons for stressing both process and product. First, there is no way to establish exact causal relationships between the actions of the board and the other participants. Secondly, as will be shown, the participants often made or make contributions that could exert influence in several directions, depending on the response of the board. Thirdly, and most significant, the focus of this thesis is the actual and potential arena within which the board exercises leadership in land use regulation.

3

An overview of the political arena within which the Fairfax County Board maneuvers will facilitate a realistic appraisal of PLUS and its attempt to exercise leadership in land use control. Most of the national, state and local developments that will be discussed in Part I emerged before the board took office. These developments will be discussed to demonstrate that the board is not an autonomous political entity, but a member of a system that affects its accomplishments. The continuing influence of other members is evident in Part II, when both growth control and general activities of the board are reviewed. Nonetheless, this evaluation centers on the leadership that the board has exhibited and may in the future enlarge upon rather than on the constraints or assistance that other actors in the political arena may provide.

The conclusion brings together Parts I and II and prospects for the future of land use contol in Fairfax County. Local leadership is an elusive dependent variable in an equation that contains few constants and independent variables. There is no easy way to solve the equation and no single solution. But it is possible to define many of the variables and approximate the nature of local leadership in development regulation.

1

Suburbanization in Fairfax County: 1960-1971

The dynamics of public regulation of growth in Fairfax County involve a demand and potential for aggressive governmental action. In pursuing its planning and land use policies, the Fairfax County Board of Supervisors is both fulfilling a commitment and seizing an opportunity to govern aggressively. The obligation was imposed by the county residents in the general election of 1971 and special election for chairman of the board in 1972.[2] The opportunity was presented by nationwide and regional developments in the area of land use control.

The demand for strong governmental regulation of growth derives from the distinctive form that suburbanization took in Fairfax County. Within twenty-five years, the largest dairy farming county in Virginia was transformed into an affluent bedroom community for professionals working in the Washington, D.C. area.[3] Since 1960, the accelerating growth rate has produced an intensity of development that has a qualitative as well as quantitative impact. Increasing requirements for public facilities and services have outstripped local capabilities and strained the resources of the county and its residents.

Trends in population, employment, taxes, land use and transportation lay the foundation for an aroused electorate frustrated by mushrooming traffic jams and spiraling property taxes. Emphasis will be placed on the 1960-71 period when the attitudes the present board is responding to were formed.

Fairfax County, like the other suburbs of the Washington, D.C. metropolitan area, experienced a post-war population explosion due to the expansion of the federal bureaucracy. From a base of roughly 96,000 inhabitants in 1950, the county more than doubled to 248,000 in 1960, and increased over 80 percent to 455,000 in 1970.[4] Since the last census, the growth rate has continued to rise, and by 1 January 1972, Fairfax had almost 503,000 residents.[5] Most of the growth resulted from in-migration. Between 1961 and 1972, it accounted for 76 percent of the increase in household population.[6]

As Fairfax County grew, its citizens became better educated, more professional, and wealthier. Residents with four years of college or more increased from 27,640, or 21 percent of the population, in 1960[7] to 69,293, or 30 percent, in 1970.[8] The proportion of workers who held white-collar jobs rose from 65 percent to 75 percent during the decade of the 1960s.[9] Despite this shift in the composition of the labor force, commutation trends showed relative continuity. In 1960, 62 percent of Fairfax workers were employed outside of the county, as compared with 61 percent in 1970.[10] Median family income

5

jumped from $8,738 to $15,707 between 1960 and 1970, a rise of roughly 70 percent using constant dollars with 1970 as the base year.[11]

Both these employment and income trends interacted with land use patterns. In 1971, 121,500 of the 257,240 acres in Fairfax County, or 47 percent of the land, was developed. Of this total amount of developed land, 37 percent consisted of residential use; 25 percent, recreational; 20 percent, rights of way, unincorporated towns, etc.; 15 percent, federal property; 2 percent, commercial; and less than 1 percent, industrial.[12] Residential development boomed in the 1960s, and the number of dwelling units increased 89 percent from 69,181 to 130,768. The composition of the housing stock changed during this period, as townhouses and apartments accounted for almost 38 percent of new construction. Single-family homes decreased as a proportion of all dwelling units from 86 percent to 75 percent between 1960 and 1970.[13]

In addition to and partly as a result of expansion, the housing stock also became more expensive. The median value of owner-occupied housing nearly doubled from $18,300 to $35,400 during the decade.[14] Average sale prices of homes rose at roughly the same rate, from $20,500 in 1960 to $40,200 in 1970.[15]

One ramification of the rising housing values is that taxes on residential property have jumped in the past thirteen years. Due to the lopsided land use pattern in Fairfax County, single family residential property bears the bulk of the fiscal burden. Of all 1971 real estate taxes collected by the county, single family dwellings accounted for 74 percent; multi-family units, 12 percent; and commerce and industry, 14 percent of the total.[16]

Because of this fiscal dependence on residential property, assessments of this type of land use have kept pace with increasing housing values. The tax rate on residential property has remained relatively stable since 1960, increasing from $3.75 per hundred dollars of assessed value (40 percent of the market value) to $4.30 in 1971. New construction and inflation in housing values have swollen the assessments base. In 1960 the assessed value of all property was roughly 349 million dollars. The 1971 figure was 1.836 billion, more than a five-fold jump.[17]

Residential development and employment and income characteristics of Fairfax County residents influenced each other in two respects. First, the emphasis on residential land use at the expense of commercial and industrial development, on the one hand, required most residents to work outside the county. On the other hand, the predominant residential land use indicates that commercial and industrial facilities were available elsewhere and that workers were willing to trade housing amenities for longer commutes.

Secondly, the generally high cost of new housing could only be afforded by upper-middle class families. This correlation emerges in a comparison of construction activity with housing values and incomes in certain parts of the county. Between 1960 and 1970, sections with the smallest change in number of housing units registered a decline in both the value of housing and family income. In contrast, those areas that experienced the largest increases in size of the housing stock also accounted for the greatest rise in residential values and family income.[18]

Although residential development more or less kept pace with population growth, highway construction lagged far behind these features of suburbanization. Between 1962 and 1972, only twenty-four miles were added to the interstate, arterial, and primary transportation network in Fairfax County, for a total of 184 miles.[19] This figure somewhat understates construction activity, as a number of major highways were widened during this period. In the meantime, use of these roads skyrocketed. Total vehicle miles traveled on this system of major highways rose from 2.1 million to 5.5 million in the ten years from 1962 to 1971.[20] As a result, "Traffic congestion on many of the county's highways exists at intolerable levels."[21] A study of the 683 miles that comprise all arterial and most collector streets in the county revealed capacity deficiencies for 21 percent of this total.[22]

Both affluence and lack of planning administration are to blame for the crowded conditions. Families can afford an average of three cars, one for every adult. In addition, suburban sprawl necessitates automobile trips for most household activities.[23] Traffic congestion makes an indelible impression on Fairfax residents, because, unlike taxes, they encounter it on a daily basis. And since highway construction funds are allocated by state and federal agencies, they have no direct way to influence expenditures. In contrast, residents may express their dissatisfaction with taxes by defeating bond issues, as they did in the sewer bond referendum of September 1970.[24]

Thus federal manpower demands, expensive housing, imbalanced land use patterns, and inadequate transportation facilities gave rise to an electoral revolt in Fairfax County. Citizens had high expectations of their local government, and when commuting became longer and taxes became higher than they considered reasonable, they registered their frustration at the polls. The present supervisors, including both the district representatives and the at-large chairman, owe their election in part to their commitment to control local growth.

2 Fairfax County's Political and Administrative Inheritance

Introduction

Due to the activities of a variety of governments, there are a growing number of techniques available for local land use regulation. However, while the range of options has multiplied in the past dozen years, constraints on local action have also increased. Before World War II, the consensus of nationwide opinion was that the initiative for development belonged with private property owners. Local jurisdictions were granted authority to exercise comprehensive planning, primarily through the ineffectual device of zoning, which served as a conduit for, rather than a check on, growth. Rapid suburbanization and the deleterious environmental effects of sprawl forced a reappraisal of this laissez-faire philosophy by citizens and officials.

As the demand for greater public participation in the development process mushroomed, the sphere of local responsibility shrank. Possessing broad and flexible authority, federal and state officials could expand their domains to encompass effective land use regulation at the expense of their local counterparts. In addition, the need for perspective and authority that extended beyond jurisdictional boundaries convinced decisionmakers in Washington, D.C. and state capitals to share in growth control at the local level. In the case of Virginia counties, conservative state legislation further restricts local regulation of private development. Thus the limitations on local ability to adopt strong land use controls must be factored into any formula that Fairfax County evolves.

Momentum for public regulation of private land use in Fairfax County as in other localities was generated by three major trends: the emphasis on planning and land use control at the federal level, the mushrooming environmental movement, and innovations in state and local development regulations across the country. Although localities generally continue to operate within the framework of zoning, they regard its purpose as legitimizing rather than functional. Having learned that zoning ordinances are weak and inflexible without local power to stage growth, progressive local governments retain them primarily to mollify conservative legislatures and courts. They concentrate instead on techniques that ensure governmental impact on local land use patterns.

The federal government has improved the capacity of local governments to manage growth by encouraging short-range, capital facilities-oriented planning. Simultaneously, these actions have also increased federal leverage over local jurisdictions. Two major examples of this federal contribution to stronger public

9

land use controls are the planning requirements of the former HUD community development programs and revenue sharing.

Concern for the environment swept localities in a tidal wave that engulfed all facets of American life. Deterioration of the environment is a problem that suburban localities are more willing but less able to confront than public housing, for example. Public opinion has propelled local officials to institute additional controls on pollutants and polluters. As in the case of community development and revenue sharing, the federal government took the initiative in developing standards and enforcement programs. But the ecology issue cannot be dealt with by individual jurisdictions. Air and water pollution ignore local boundaries, and both federal intervention and regional cooperation are needed to protect the quality of life in localities.

Development pressure, most intense in the suburbs, was the third trend propelling localities to devise new techniques for controlling growth. Two major features distinguish conventional and innovative land use controls: the public attitude toward development and the locus of administrative decisionmaking. Basically, conventional land use controls, epitomized by zoning, impose a burden of proof on localities to justify restricting the use of land. This presumptive validity is reversed under innovative techniques, which require the developer to prove the desirability of growth, often to state and regional, as well as local, agencies.

Whereas once growth was viewed as natural and the conventional public role consisted of reacting to private initiative, progressive localities reject development as a foregone conclusion and have originated programs to guide future growth. An operational corollary of this new orientation is public influence over the timing of growth. Using innovative techniques, governments can address the question of when development should occur, in addition to what is to be built, how, and where.

When the initiative for development was in private hands, local government had sole responsibility for implementing feeble regulatory measures prescribed in state enabling legislation. As more and more authority is transferred to public hands, other levels of government participate in decisions relating to the timing of growth. In all efforts to augment public control over land use, local officials find that they invariably must share authority wrested from private interests with federal, state, or regional counterparts.

Two examples of local land use controls that contribute to public phasing of development are: requirement of environmental impact statements (EIS), and adequate public facilities (APF) legislation. The former protects the existing physical and, in some cases, socio-economic setting from new development, while the latter ensures the necessary amenities for future residents at a reasonable public cost. Both devices treat growth as conditional depending on governmental assessment of potential adverse effects and feasibility in land use and fiscal terms.

The potential for local governments to participate in fundamental decisions affecting growth has thus been expanded by federal emphasis on short-range planning and balanced residential development, nationwide interest in protecting the physical environment, and innovative land use controls adopted by states and localities. The key to increased public regulation of development is realistic planning that deals with human needs in concrete terms. Whether the subject is low and moderate-income housing or storm drainage facilities, a government must justify its goals and regulatory measures by preparing comprehensive development plans for capital improvements and other public amenities. This reliance on practical planning has given the public sector the right to exercise an enlarged role in the development process. How the additional authority is divided among the competing levels of government remains to be determined. It is certain, nonetheless, that more effective means of controlling growth are becoming available to localities.

Although the demand and potential for increased public regulation of development are present in Fairfax County, these two elements alone cannot effect the board's goals. A third element, vital to successful implementation of its planning and land use program, is the board's capacity for leadership. By embracing a new philosophy and policymaking style, the present supervisors have redefined their role relative to both the county administrative staff and the housing industry. Board control over these two groups, which previously assumed primary responsibility for land use decisions, requires modified operations. Before detailing these operations and possible additional changes, it is important to analyze institutional constraints on board action. As Virginia is not a home rule state, there are severe restrictions on the powers of localities. In addition, recent developments in Fairfax County government affect the current board's status. Consequently, the Fairfax County supervisors confront indigenous circumstances that directly influence their ability to lead.

Fairfax County is experiencing a crisis of leadership, precipitated by the present board's effort to disassociate itself from its predecessors and to undertake a novel approach to growth control. Its radical behavior has confused some county agencies, angered many developers, and exasperated some of the citizens. Due to the negative reactions of these key groups, the board is realizing that, although it is the apex of the governmental pyramid, it is neither independent nor omnipotent. An industry counterattack has made the board vulnerable and convinced it to mute its abrasive assault on past procedures.

Despite the setbacks that the board has suffered, its ability to challenge the established system attests to the flexibility of the local political and administrative fabric. The board was able to create a fluid situation that demanded a redefinition of the functions of the governing body, administrative staff, and housing industry. In initiating this reassessment, it is influenced by restrictions imposed by the state legislature and recent trends in Fairfax County government.

The political and administrative legacy that the present Board of Supervisors inherited is a source of both strength and weakness for leadership in local government. Part of this legacy derives from the general assembly and part originates in Fairfax County. Key precedents that impinge on the board's attempt to lead the county government, particularly with respect to planning and land use, will be assessed. At the state level, the subjects comprise: limited authority accorded to counties with overall responsibility vested in the Board of Supervisors, prescribed planning and land use control techniques available to counties, and provisions of the urban county executive form of government. In the local context, analysis will focus on the continuous reorganization and fragmentation of the bureaucracy, rapid turnover on the Board of Supervisors and in the office of county executive, and the pre-existing system of planning and land use control.

Virginia State Enabling Legislation

General Powers Delegated to Counties

The Virginia General Assembly has delegated limited responsibilities to localities and particularly to the counties that contain most of the state's population. Local authority is, however, concentrated in relatively few governmental entities. Unlike many local governments, Virginia counties are required to share responsibility with only a handful of authorities, commissions, and boards. In the case of planning and land use, state enabling legislation assigns responsibility, apart from functions performed by administrative agencies, to the following governmental entities: planning commission, board of zoning appeals, school board, and park, sewer, and water authorities.

But the county government nonetheless retains substantial control over their operations. In the first place, the chief officials of these bodies are appointed exclusively by the board of supervisors, except for the school superintendent, who must be confirmed by the State Board of Education, and the members of the board of zoning appeals, who are appointed by the circuit court. Secondly, the three authorities are optional and can only be created through a local referendum. Fairfax County presently has park and water authorities. Thirdly, only the water authority, whose source of revenue is user fees, is financially independent of the county government. Budgets for all other boards, commissions, and other advisory bodies beyond the county executive's jurisdiction must be approved by the Board of Supervisors.[25]

In addition to specifying these governmental entities, the general assembly has given counties broad latitude to perform their prescribed duties. Localities determine the organization of their administrative staff, which consists mainly of career bureaucrats and some appointed senior officials. They may also establish advisory bodies, staffed by citizens, public servants, and experts, to address specific county issues on a temporary or permanent basis. Thus delegation of local authority is, with few exceptions, an option available to the county government.

Within this state-imposed framework of restricted and yet relatively consolidated responsibility, the board of supervisors is the chief legislative, executive, and administrative body in the county. This dominant status can both undermine and fortify a board's capacity for leadership.

There are two ways that the board's supremacy can detract from its ability to lead the county. On the one hand, it may assume so much responsibility that it is overwhelmed and can neither become fully informed about all vital issues nor devote sufficient time to them. This tendency is exacerbated by the low salary that members of the board receive. State law sets a $10,000 salary maximum for urban county supervisors.[26] This ceiling requires board members who support families to hold another position in order to earn an adequate income and thus spend less time on county business.

On the other hand, board control over governmental functions, most of which are concentrated in the administrative agencies, traces a clear chain of accountability that leads to the board. Local politicians, who are accessible to constituents and sensitive to their scrutiny, are more visible and vulnerable if they have clear-cut jurisdiction. A board of supervisors might tend toward conservatism under these circumstances.

Despite these potential drawbacks, the supervisors' preeminence can have a positive effect on their leadership capabilities. The board exercises considerable influence on local government with final decisionmaking responsibility in general county affairs and in most aspects of planning and land use control. Its legislative powers are complete: only the board can adopt local ordinances and resolutions. The board is also the executive head of the county through its authority to establish policies. Finally, the board resolves major county administrative issues and impacts on general administration by selecting the county executive and approving the appointment of the deputy county executive and department heads.

Planning and Land Use Control

The powers of a Virginia board to regulate development range from meager to extensive depending on how state enabling legislation relating to planning and land use control is interpreted. A literal reading of the state code indicates that a county has at its disposal a limited number of techniques, some of which must be administered in prescribed ways. For instance, a board of supervisors must establish a planning commission in order to enact a zoning ordinance. Also, to allow special exceptions and variances, a county must create a board of zoning appeals, which has sole jurisdiction over these components of the local zoning ordinance.[27] The general assembly has thus given counties the right to adopt certain traditional means of land use control and placed some constraints on their application.

Virginia has restricted the administration of zoning because it is the land use control device that local governments rely upon most heavily. In contrast, the requirements for subdivision regulation, a measure whose full potential has not been exploited, are much more vague and accord substantial discretion to the county governing body. A relatively undeveloped Virginia county that was willing to shift the emphasis of its land use control program away from zoning could acquire greater authority to guide growth. Since the pattern of development is set when land is subdivided into lots, a county must contain enough raw land to profit from increased reliance on subdivision control. Fairfax County is in this position, as over half of the county is undeveloped. It has not, however, taken the initiative to expand this type of land use control.

The crux of the liberal justification for broader powers is the fact that the general assembly has not dealt specifically with innovative land use controls. As long as the county conforms to guidelines upheld by courts in other states, its actions are legal. Notwithstanding, it is crucial for the county to reinforce its position, which is naturally tenuous due to the absence of home rule in Virginia. Furthermore, judicial decisions in one state are not binding on another state. As no cases dealing with novel growth regulations have appeared in Virginia, the courts may accept or reject precedents set in California, New York, and other states whose courts have ruled favorably on these types of measures.

One logical way to mitigate adverse judicial reaction is to base innovative techniques on traditional elements of land use regulation. This approach has worked well in other states. For instance, the comprehensive plan and capital improvements program, which had ambiguous status and played a largely ineffectual role in conventional public regulation of land use, have been reconstituted to form the foundation of vigorous control programs. Thus by relying on semantics and legal technicalities, a Virginia county may attempt to introduce novel forms of development control.

The Urban County Executive Form of Government

The Fairfax County Board's capacity for leadership depends not only on state enabling legislation dealing with general county government and a liberal interpretation of county planning and land use powers. It also relies on the particular form of government that the county has adopted.

In the late 1950s, Fairfax officials determined that the existing governmental system could not meet the needs of an urbanizing jurisdiction. There was concern about future incorporation within the county. The growth rate was expected to give a number of communities the necessary population to become towns or independent cities. County officials wanted to avoid fragmented administration of public services and a multiplicity of local governments. They also wanted to promote professionalism within the bureaucracy by strengthening the office of county executive and the career civil service system.

Despite the interest in modernization, both citizens and local politicians remained attached to some traditional practices, notably district representation and state maintenance of roads. All of these goals and attitudes were reflected in the governmental form that was created in the early 1960s.

A Fairfax County request prompted the general assembly to devise the urban county executive form, which was approved in a 1966 local referendum and took effect on 1 January 1968.[28] Provisions of this form both contribute to and detract from the board's ability to lead the county in an assertive manner. Three features of the urban county executive form shape the orientation and functioning of the board, both collectively and as individual members. They are: district representation on the board and major appointed bodies, lack of staggered terms for board members, and the part-time status accorded to the board.

Since 1968 the Fairfax County Board of Supervisors has been a nine-member body, composed of eight district representatives and an at-large chairman. After the previous chairman resigned due to a lack of responsibility, the largely ceremonial function of the at-large position was amended. As a result of county code changes, the chairman not only presides over meetings, but also participates fully in discussions, votes and other board business. His or her countywide political base, however, sets the chairman apart from the other members who are accountable to a particular segment of the electorate. Each of the eight district supervisors represents an average of 70,000 persons. As a consequence, district members receive approximately 250 constituent requests per month.[29] These requests range from complaints about broken street lights to petitions for the county to assume responsibility for fire and rescue services in a community.

District representation also characterizes the school board and planning commission. When a vacancy occurs, or a term expires, the district supervisor nominates a constituent to serve on each of these influential bodies, while the chairman nominates an at-large member. Each nominee must be approved by the entire board, and it is customary to appoint proposed representatives.

Political and administrative ramifications of district representation can either promote or hinder board planning and land use control leadership. The accessibility of district supervisors provides a vital channel for citizen participation. This outlet is critical, because Fairfax County contains a dynamic network of community organizations that demand involvement in local government.[30] There is the possibility, however, that members may emphasize district matters to the neglect of countywide issues. A further complication arises if the at-large chairman purports to represent all county residents but expresses less than a consensus of board opinion. Such political pressure may have the positive effect of encouraging more parochial district supervisors to broaden their perspective.

While district representation creates the problem of weighing constituent against countywide priorities, the absence of staggered terms places a strain on the entire governmental system. This strain may produce both beneficial and harmful results. Since all board members are elected simultaneously for four-year terms, the board can consist of predominantly new members. This situation has existed in the recent past. Anxious to fulfill election pledges, new members may be more critical of the status quo and eager to bring about change than veterans.

First-term supervisors are often, however, inexperienced in politics, parliamentary procedure, and administration. They may not know how to deal with the bureaucracy or interest groups, and they may not care to learn. In addition, they are usually concerned with making a name for themselves, especially members with more ambitious political aspirations. Because interaction with staff or special interests is generally low-keyed or behind the scenes, it would not yield publicity dividends as much as more visible activities, like speeches to civic associations.

No matter how active a role the supervisor may want to play, the general assembly has allotted salary and staff designed for a part-time member. The enabling legislation is nevertheless more flexible with regard to the staff assigned to members than with their own salary. Under the urban county executive form, each supervisor may receive no more than $10,000 annually and may hire only one secretary. Provisions covering general county government are more open-ended, however, and allow supervisors as much assistance as they need.[31] The Fairfax County board, by adhering to the general stipulation, may expand the staff of individual members.

Despite the impediment of low salary and limited assistance, most supervisors manage to devote a full work week to constituent and countywide affairs. They cannot, however, consistently work around the clock, because of their obligations to other jobs and to their families. While this less than total commitment to their public office may limit their activities, it may also give them additional perspective on county government and their role. Like district representation and single-year elections, the part-time status envisioned for supervisors can make them parochial and irreverent toward conventional politicking. These potential characteristics can operate independently, reinforce, or counterbalance each other. Depending on how this parochialism and irreverence are used, they can either strengthen or weaken board leadership.

The potential that the state legislature created for leadership by the Fairfax County supervisors is thus flexible. Provisions relating to general county and urban county executive government and local planning and land use offer them sufficient options to carry out their mandate for activism. The Virginia code contains enough ambiguities and loopholes to accommodate enterprising supervisors.

General Fairfax County Government during the 1960s

Administrative Reorganization

Fairfax County's governing body is not solely influenced, however, by activities in Richmond. The political and administrative environment that affects its leadership ability also includes local patterns of governmental behavior. Three features of the local landscape particularly affect the present board's leadership capacity: governmental reorganization and administrative fragmentation, turnover in the board and position of county executive, and previous board response to development pressures. Furthermore, no governing body operates in a policymaking vacuum. In the case of Fairfax County boards that served from 1960 to 1972, the planning staff, county executive, and housing industry assumed shifting responsibility in shaping planning and land use policies.

As the pace of urbanization accelerated in the 1960s, county officials realized that local government had to respond to changing conditions. Continuous study and evaluation of county government produced a series of governmental reorganizations, accompanied by administrative fragmentation. This refinement process and its effect on administration have both fostered and stymied board leadership. Some of the modifications were initiated by the board and others by the county executive. So to a certain extent, the supervisors were the authors of their fate.

The first major governmental reorganization took place from 1968 to 1970, when the recommendations of Cresap, Pagett, and McCormick, a management consulting firm, were implemented. The consultant study, directed by George C. Kelley, was commissioned to adapt the urban county executive form to specific conditions in Fairfax County. As the state code only specified some governmental functions and agencies, the county was responsible for developing a complete administrative structure and making the transition to the new organization.[32]

Kelley started at the top of the administrative hierarchy and then made major changes in the development-related departments. In 1968, he established two deputy county executive positions to replace the single slot that existed previously. One deputy county executive handled administration, and the other planning and financial management. When he created these positions, he arranged to be appointed deputy county executive for planning and financial management. In this capacity, he expanded the data and management analysis activities of the county.[33]

His proposals for a Department of County Development (DCD) and a revamped Department of Public Works (DPW) were carried out in 1969. County Development was formed by removing zoning-related functions from the Planning Division and public works functions involving private development from Public Works.[34] This arrangement is a prime example of administrative fragmentation. On the one hand, both Planning and County Development reviewed rezoning applications to ensure that the proposals conform to Planning's long-range comprehensive plans and County Development's short-range development plans. On the other hand, Public Works and County Development performed comparable engineering, design, and administrative functions, but for different clients. Public Works served the county government and residents, and County Development, private developers.

While restructuring the planning and land use agencies, Kelley also turned to the social service agencies. As in the case of the development-related departments, Kelley performed a complete overhaul on the health, social, and community service departments. He added new agencies and personnel, replaced some senior staff, and also changed the names of agencies to reflect broader responsibilities.[35]

Additional modifications of the bureaucracy occurred in 1971, when Kelley became county executive. Most dealt with the county executive's office, planning and financial management, and public works. He abolished the position of deputy county executive for planning and financial management and created a general deputy county executive and a management and budget office under the county executive.[36] He also made himself director of the DPW after firing the previous director, who was accused of issuing sewer permits that exceeded treatment plant capacity.[37]

Continuous administrative alterations impeded board leadership from 1968 to 1971 because George C. Kelley, Jr. was fashioning a bureaucracy that achieved his personal and philosophical goals. He assumed that growth equalled progress and proceeded to ensure efficient development. Most of his reforms did not directly affect board functions, and the supervisors acceded to suggestions that required their approval. During this period, the supervisors were divided on the issue of growth regulation and generally compromised on a middle-of-the-road position. Their moderation invited Kelley to usurp the initiative in policymaking.

Turnover in the Board of Supervisors

While the responsibility for bureaucratic restructuring lies with the board, the initiative for turnover in the board rests with the electorate. And the voters of Fairfax County have exercised their prerogative to reject incumbents with apparent verve since 1960. Perhaps owing to their predominantly junior status, previous boards pursued a conservative course in dealing with the county executive. As in the case of administrative reorganization, personalities and actions determine the precise effect of past board and county executive tenure on the present board's leadership capacity.

Fifteen persons served as Fairfax County supervisors between 1960 and 1972. Four elections were held during this period, three general and one special. In each of the general elections a majority of new members was voted into office: five in 1959 and four in 1963 for the seven-member boards, and six in 1967 for the nine-member board. The board that took office in 1964 had the largest proportion of incumbents, three out of seven, but it was rocked by a scandal that changed its composition in mid-term. Two members who had been reelected in 1963 were indicted for accepting bribes and removed from office. Replacements were elected in a special election to serve for the remainder of the regular term. These events left only one incumbent on the 1964 board. Neither supervisor who took office in 1966 won reelection in the 1967 general election.[38]

As a result of this rapid turnover, the average tenure for these board members was 4.8 years. A majority of eight supervisors served a single term during the 1960-1971 period, while three served a maximum of two terms. In the recent past, therefore, the length of service for the members of the Board of Supervisors has not been long.

This high turnover rate has the potential to both assist and hinder board leadership. Because the majority of members on the board were new since 1960, this presented an opportunity to innovate. They are neither associated with established practices nor accountable to interest groups that have promoted pet projects. But action requires knowledge, and inexperienced politicians might adopt a wait-and-see attitude until they are able to make a more informed decision. Previous boards tended toward the conservative style.

With regard to the county executive, these predominantly novice boards played a generally passive role. Carleton C. Massey was appointed county executive during the 1950s and continued to serve throughout the following decade. He left office by personal choice in 1970. Upon his retirement, the board immediately selected George C. Kelley, Jr., then deputy county executive for planning and financial management, as his successor.[39]

This rapid change in the office of county executive both encouraged and discouraged board leadership. As in the case of board tenure, personalities and the goals of the board and county executive were pivotal. Massey was an old-time, conservative county executive who fulfilled the will of the board when expressed and carried on business as usual when it was not. Thus he supported the efforts of the 1964-67 board to reorganize the County government by hiring Kelley as his deputy.

Kelley was the antithesis of Massey in background, orientation, and style. Although they made him county executive, the 1968-71 supervisors did not find that Kelley promoted their leadership aspirations. In the first place, the board's desire to lead was relatively weak, or at least poorly expressed. Secondly, Kelley was himself a newcomer and could offer little guidance to county politics beyond the bureaucratic changes he introduced. Finally, Kelley was a retired military officer who evidently saw himself, rather than the board, as the leader of the government. While in office he expanded his and not the supervisors' authority. The contrast between Massey and Kelley illustrates the range of impact that the county executive's experience and approach can have on the potential for board leadership.

3 Fairfax County Planning and Land Use Control: 1960-1971

Introduction

The three boards that governed Fairfax County from 1960 to 1972 conducted most of their development-related business in an administrative context. While they adopted master plans and multi-family housing criteria, their policies are contained primarily in discussion of individual rezoning applications. A distinct pattern emerges from a study of board rezoning decisions on proposed developments during the 1960s.[a]

First, the housing industry provided the impetus for elaboration of planning and rezoning criteria. Secondly, Planning and later County Development staff responded to industry initiative by modifying the master plans and zoning ordinance. Finally, the boards never paid full attention to criteria developed by staff. Rather, their concern with stipulated requirements was equivocal. Amendments to the county zoning ordinance between 1960 and 1970 indicate general board deferral to industry proposals. Nonetheless, the supervisors' administrative and legislative record also reveals increased sophistication in dealing with

[a]The source of this research is the dissertation of John Hysom, a former Fairfax County employee. A brief explanation of his approach and findings will establish the reliability and limitations of his work. Hysom analyzed 191 single-family and 131 multi-family residential zoning cases decided by the supervisors from 1960 through 1969. Most of these cases involved parcels of ten acres or more. Based on tape recordings and written summaries of board meetings and county publications, he isolated criteria for rezoning applications. He evaluated board adherence to these criteria and to planning staff and Planning Commission recommendations regarding the individual rezoning cases.

There are two flaws in Hysom's methodology. First, as he admits, the single-family rezoning criteria "were not formally defined or formally adopted by the Board of County Supervisors.[40] As a result, these criteria may not have guided decisions but perhaps only justified them. Irregular application of these standards support the contention that their primary purpose was to rationalize board decisions. Only three of the six single-family and four of the ten multi-family criteria were followed in over 50 percent of all cases. Furthermore, the most frequently followed criterion was only adhered to 79 percent of the time.[41]

Secondly, standards for both single-family and multi-family housing originated in staff reports or district comprehensive plans. Some of these documents were formally adopted by the Board of Supervisors and others were not. Hysom applied criteria developed under one board (whether or not they were officially adopted) to the succeeding board, if no new prerequisites for development were established. For instance, he evaluated the multi-family rezoning decisions of the 1968-72 board based on the standards contained in the apartment study approved by the 1964-68 board. While these defects impair the utility of his statistics, Hysom's research is a reasonable measure of trends in board planning and land use decisions over the decade.

planning and land use control. In particular, they exhibited an expanding awareness of the limitations that traditional zoning imposed on public efforts to regulate growth.

Evolution of the Local Housing Industry

The Fairfax County housing industry became a formidable force in local development as a result of three factors. The first and perhaps most pivotal was the continuous demand for housing in the Washington, D.C. metropolitan area. Employment opportunities in the federal government and easy FHA mortgage terms attracted returning World War II veterans to the local suburbs. Population increase based primarily on immigration has persisted. This favorable economic climate has motivated the industry to attempt to maintain its dominant role in residential development.

The sound market for housing stimulated the second factor that strengthened the industry's position: large-scale and professional residential development. During the late 1940s and early 1950s, the typical Fairfax County developer was a native property owner who wanted to convert farm land or open space to residential use. Most subdivisions were small and densities were low. The majority of dwellings were single-family homes, although some duplex and garden apartment units were also built.

Increased accessibility to Fairfax County and rising land prices in the more developed suburbs bordering the District of Columbia stimulated large-scale building in Fairfax County. Construction of I-95, the arterial highway that bisects southeastern Fairfax, encouraged native Virginia builders who had concentrated their operations in Arlington to expand to Fairfax. In turn, completion of I-495, the region's circumferential expressway in suburban Virginia and Maryland, attracted developers in Montgomery and Prince George's Counties to Fairfax. These newcomers were development corporations who had the financial and technical resources to undertake larger and denser housing projects. Expertise, an easy lending market, and high land costs produced a boom in high-rise and other types of apartment construction in the county during the mid-1960s.

The housing industry's political clout is the third major factor enabling it to challenge the board's growth control policies. This factor is interrelated with the economic climate and industry operations. Construction is the second largest private industry in the metropolitan area, and this economic power translates into political leverage. Initially this leverage was applied in the administrative branch of county government. As will be shown, the rezoning criteria and new land use categories adopted during the 1960s reflect industry priorities.

Developers also stand on firm ground with respect to the judicial system. On the one hand, previous county accommodation to growth pressure set precedents that support industry claims. On the other hand, the development community has remained predominantly local and thus avoids a carpetbagger label.[42]

These three ingredients of consumer demand, corporate operations, and traditional development practices produced the housing industry's prominent position in land use control.

**Private Stimulus for Refinement
of Planning and Rezoning Criteria**

Private sector desire for change in the development process provided the impetus for refinement of public land use regulation.[43] Notably in the rezoning guidelines, but also in the staging of comprehensive plan revision, pressure from the housing industry motivated county actions. Certain amendments to the zoning ordinance and the order in which district master plans were drawn up exemplify the influence of developers and property owners.

The Residential Planned Community (RPC) and Planned Development Housing and Commercial (PDH, PDC) zoning classifications were created in response to industry requests for more flexible development regulations. The RPC category is particularly striking, since it appeared at a time when board planning and land use activities generally showed little sophistication. It resulted from the efforts of a single developer, Robert E. Simon, who needed its alternate density, clustering, and mixed land use provisions to build his new town of Reston.[44]

In 1962 the county had a brief and vague comprehensive plan that could hardly serve as a guide for public decisions. To supplement its meager planning resources, the board endorsed the Year 2000 Plan for the metropolitan Washington area devised by the National Capital Planning Commission (NCPC).[45] This plan, however, proved inappropriate for most of Fairfax County on theoretical grounds (not to mention the practical grounds documented by William H. Whyte in *The Last Landscape*). Topographic features, especially drainage patterns, precluded development along major transportation corridors, as proposed by NCPC. The fall line gave rise to a network that runs perpendicular to the main highways and thus required filling in the wedges that the planners had reserved for open space.[46]

In contrast to their slight interest in governmental planning, the board approved of the private planning process integral to the development of Reston. Because of Simon's new town, the supervisors made an isolated leap forward in land use control that was unequaled until the adoption of incentive zoning nearly a decade later. The planned development zones, which accord density bonuses to developers who install public facilities, reflect concern over rising land prices during the late 1960s. As land costs increased, developers sought means of limiting this expense. An obvious alternative was high-rise and cluster development, which incentive zoning promoted. The planned development categories thus responded to the demands of a broad spectrum of the housing industry, rather than of a single developers, as in the case of Reston.

The influence of the housing industry was further evident in the order in which planning district plans were prepared. In accordance with state enabling legislation, the board scheduled a revision of the 1958 comprehensive plan in 1963. To facilitate the updating process, the board departed from the approach of a countywide plan and divided the county into fourteen planning districts.[47]

Pressure for development was apparently the foundation of the priority system for completing these district plans. The earliest plans, adopted by the board in mid-1963, covered the eastern portion of the county that was experiencing the most rapid suburbanization. During 1964 and 1965, plans dealing with eastern and southern portions of the county were approved. Availability of transportation facilities, particularly I-95, partly accounted for the high levels of development activity in the Annandale, Springfield, and Jefferson districts. Finally, plans for the northern, southern, and western portions, which were less accessible and had fewer public facilities, were prepared.

From 1960 to 1968, primary responsibility for devising evaluation standards for residential rezoning was assumed by the county planning staff. The supervisors, however, injected their opinions in the process, since they diverged from staff recommendations on rezoning applications 17 percent of the time[48] and often ignored many of the established standards. But in terms of delineating policy, the Planning Division exerted a dominant influence. An example of this staff role is its *Multiple Family Housing Study*, made in 1964. The study outlined six components considered essential to support apartment projects: water, sewer, transportation, shopping, and public facilities, including schools, parks, and recreation areas.[49] Although the board disregarded these criteria in numerous cases,[50] they never proposed alternative guidelines.

Board/staff relations remained fairly constant over the decade of the 1960s: no major shifts in board concurrence or disagreement with staff recommendations emerged. Yet the forum for developer/staff interaction changed. Until 1969, the Planning Division combined planning and zoning functions, and the DPW handled facilities such as water and sewer lines. As detailed above, the DCD was created by transferring responsibility for zoning and public facilities serving private development to the new agency. This administration reorganization produced the DCD, whose sole purpose was to deal with property owners and developers.

The existence of this department presupposes that growth will occur and thus undermines public challenge of development. Furthermore, because County Development staff performs services for developers, such as site plan review and building inspection, it can only regulate the quality and not the quantity of development. The staff report prepared on every rezoning application illustrates the input that County Development makes. Originally prepared by the Planning Division, the staff report became a joint Planning and County Development responsibility. When the two departments disagree, which happens about one-fourth of the time, County Development makes the final decision.[51] This arrangement places a different perspective on growth regulation. Whereas the Planning staff focuses on the broader impact of the proposed development, County Development staff concentrates on technical aspects of the individual project. Because the locus for staff evaluation of rezoning requests changed, the criteria acquired a different emphasis. They became more developer-oriented.

The Boards' Role in Development Regulation

There are two hypothetical explanations for the failure of these three boards to exercise more active and direct leadership in growth regulation. On the one hand, they may not have wanted to take responsibility for patterns of development. The three criteria most often followed by the boards in single and multi-family rezoning requests were availability of sewer and water and conformance with adjacent property. These are deterministic and conservative conditions that lie beyond each board's control. The location of water and sewer lines and distribution of land uses in effect when these boards governed were the result of decisions made by preceding county officials.

On the other hand, and closely related to the first reason, these boards may not have wanted to commit themselves to specific policies. Although the absence of valid guidelines hampers decisionmaking, it also provides the decisionmaker with greater latitude. Patterns of board adherence to accessibility and shopping criteria support this contention. The record indicates that the less explicit the criteria, the more closely they were followed. Availability of transportation and commercial facilities were standards applied most often by the board that served from 1960 to 1964. Under the two succeeding boards, their application declined sharply. At the same time, these criteria were expressed in progressively greater detail. This trend may have resulted from a delayed staff reaction to board pronouncements, rather than from board avoidance of definitive guidelines. But there was obviously a board penchant for casual standards and an informal decisionmaking process that afforded more discretion.

Despite the three boards' refusal to assume maximum control over growth regulation, their deviation from established staff criteria demonstrates positive, if not primary, involvement. Six basic criteria were developed for both single and multi-family housing, and four additional criteria were set for apartments. The common guidelines consisted of sewer, water, and educational facilities, conformance with adjacent property, compliance with adopted master plans, and soil conditions. The separate multi-family standards covered transportation, drainage facilities, parks and recreation areas, and shopping facilities. Table 3-1 indicates the frequency with which all three boards adhered to the established criteria.

These data suggest acceptance of growth as inevitable and accommodation to private development pressures. The boards applied the more deterministic criteria with greater consistency, but also relied heavily on external factors. A supportive board posture toward the housing industry is also borne out by the rezoning decisions of these three boards. On the average, 89 percent of the single-family and 94 percent of the multi-family housing projects in the research sample were approved from 1960 to 1969.[52]

Although these supervisors consistently provided for private residential development, they also progressively expanded their protection of the general welfare. Gradually, they appeared to modify their conception of growth from a privately claimed right to a publicly granted privilege. A review of major multi-family residential use districts adopted during the 1960s illustrates the increasing sophistication and sensitivity of these boards.

In 1960 the Board of Supervisors was evidently ill-equipped to handle multi-family housing rezoning applications. Like many suburban jurisdictions

Table 3-1
Residential Zoning Criteria in Fairfax County (Rezoning Cases Approved, 1960-1969)

Criterion	Proportion of Cases Where Criterion Applied	
	Single-Family (%)	Multi-Family (%)
Adequate sewer	79	66
Conform with adjacent land use	71	62
Adequate water	59	70
Comply with existing county plans	40	47
Adequate schools	31	58
Soil conditions	13	33
Adequate access*		49
Nearby shopping*		42
Adequate drainage*		15
Adequate parks and recreation*		14

*Applied only to multi-family residential development

Source: John L. Hysom, Jr. "An Evaluation of the Planning and Zoning Criteria Used for Allocating Land for Residential Purposes in Fairfax County, Virginia," (The American University, Doctoral Dissertation, second draft May 15, 1973) pp. 139, 180.

across the country, Fairfax County was concerned with protecting its single-family character, but lacked standards for evaluating the feasibility or appropriateness of higher density residential uses. The original zoning ordinance, adopted in 1941 and amended slightly in 1956, permitted apartments in the general business district. The ordinance required the Board of Supervisors to grant a special exception for their construction in the urban residential district after the Planning Commission reviewed the application.[53] But demand for multi-family housing necessitated refining this antiquated provision of the law.

Consequently, the board imposed a moratorium on apartment rezoning cases for the first nine months of 1960, while the Planning Division prepared an apartment study.[54] Based on the staff report and later development proposals, the board added a variety of multi-family residential categories to the zoning ordinance during its term: high-rise and garden apartments, townhouses, residential planned communities, and cluster/alternative density housing.

Under the next board, the zoning ordinance was further amended to permit medium-rise apartments, planned apartment developments, and townhouses at densities of five or ten per acre using conventional placement or clusters. Finally, the board that served from 1968 to 1972 extended the RPC and cluster options still further. It established a planned development housing category, which provides for a mixture of residential uses, and permitted townhouses in high-rise and garden apartment zones.[55]

Thus these three boards pursued two different approaches designed to achieve a common purpose: greater public control over multi-family housing development. On the one hand, they increased the types of allowed multi-family residential uses and added detailed specifications for the developments and their surrounding neighborhoods. On the other hand, they created multi-family housing categories that gave them broader latitude to deal with developers on an individual basis. Rezoning became more of a negotiation process, where the public and private parties engaged in bargaining and compromise. Traditional zoning, floating zones, and incentive zoning allowed these boards to expand their regulation of residential land use.

Conclusion

Although the three boards that served from 1960 to 1972 became progressively more aware of the need to regulate growth and adopted more sophisticated controls, they left the initiative for development in private hands. They acquiesced to most housing industry requests for both diversified residential uses and rezonings to higher densities. They also delegated major responsibility for defining residential rezoning criteria to the Planning Division and later the DCD. Their primary response to the mushrooming growth pressures was decision-making in a case-by-case review of rezoning applications. Most of their planning and land use policies were implied; few were enunciated.

This twelve year record contains both assets and liabilities for the present board in its efforts to assume leadership in planning and land use control. Drawbacks predominate, notably the laissez faire attitude that fostered private impetus for development. The previous boards nonetheless established precedents for public regulation through administration, such as requirements for adequate public facilities and compliance with comprehensive plans. Despite frequent disregard for these guidelines, their existence and the trend of gradually strengthened governmental control over growth reinforces the present board's attempt to extend that control still further.

Part II: Public Management of Growth in Fairfax County since 1972

Introduction to Part II

The national, state, and local participants discussed in Part I have the potential to promote or constrain the present board's efforts to regulate growth. They can neither guarantee nor prevent the emergence of aggressive local leadership, nor determine the accomplishments of local leaders. Their precise influence in the political arena depends on the Board of Supervisors. Thus in Part II, the emphasis shifts from potential impact on the board to its actual initiative in land use control.

The Fairfax County supervisors are change agents. Whereas most government consists of routine operations, innovation in growth regulation is their hallmark. This role requires a special type of leadership, which has extraordinary institutional ramifications. In the atmosphere that the board has created, leadership is an earned rather than imputed trait.

Ordinarily the terms "leader," "chief political official," and "head of government" are synonymous. Leaders are those individuals who have final decisionmaking authority. This definition assumes that people who have authority exercise it and receive support so that their decisions are carried out. This assumption cannot be applied to the Fairfax County Board's growth control activities, because the governing body is trying to redistribute authority in this highly controversial and volatile area.

Under these circumstances, leadership connotes the ability to act and inspire others to follow. Whether or not the titular heads are actually leaders is determined by their performance. It will be shown that the Fairfax supervisors only demonstrated an ability to act in their first year in office. They became leaders, in the special sense explained above, when they formulated PLUS and thus demonstrated an ability to inspire as well.

The board's commitment to change growth regulation through action and inspiration will be assessed in the framework of administrative policymaking. Because it is both attempting to exercise a special type of leadership and reallocate responsibility for land use control, the board must modify routine governance. The ordinary governmental process consists of three phases: policy formulation, program delineation, and implementation. In the case of the Fairfax County Board, however, a fourth phase must be added: legitimization. Where the standards for official policy and the boundaries of the public domain are definitive and accepted, there is no need to justify specific decisions. But when traditional goals and roles are challenged and public administration is in transition, legitimization becomes an integral phase of administrative policymaking. The supervisors have promoted such a situation and are therefore obligated to legitimatize their innovations.

When they first took office, the supervisors did not seem to recognize this obligation. Apparently they equated their election mandate with blanket legitimacy. They evidently misjudged their position, because their initial policies by no means met with unanimous local approval. In the wake of judicial rebuffs and public criticism, they proposed PLUS. This program addresses all four phases of administrative policymaking. Along with its strengths, PLUS contains deficiencies, many of which will be detailed.

Before analyzing the board's performance in planning and land use, its general administrative procedures will be reviewed. The way the board handles overall countywide and district level business affects its treatment of development regulation. One outstanding accomplishment of the board applies to all its activities, growth control and others. It has managed to politicize county administration to an extraordinary extent. Even though the county executive is its appointee, it has swollen the number of advisory bodies, such as commissions and councils. These governmental entities are directly responsible to the board, unlike the administrative agencies that report to the county executive.

The advisory bodies in effect constitute a counterbureaucracy, which decreases board reliance on staff in many instances. They are both an effect and cause of tension between the supervisors and the former and present county executive. This tension is evident in the preparation and conduct of board meetings and in other relations among the board, administrative staff, and advisory bodies. These aspects of county government in large part determine board and staff efficiency and effectiveness and thus merit particular scrutiny.

4

General Governance by the Board of Supervisors

Introduction

As Fairfax County's governing body, the Board of Supervisors influences the tone, direction, and pace of public administration. Because growth control is a major local responsibility and Fairfax's primary preoccupation, the board expends much of its energy on zoning, planning, and other land use-related matters. There are two main vehicles for the board to pursue these activities with its administrative staff and citizens: weekly board meetings and advisory bodies. These vehicles contain two features, one present and the other anticipated, which require special attention in order to facilitate implementation of PLUS.

First of all, weekly board meetings, the major forum for collective action by the governing body, are inefficient. The sessions begin in mid-morning and usually last through the evening and into the next day. Their length results from the volume of business that the board handles and an emphasis on fact-finding and position stating rather than decisionmaking during meetings.

Secondly, PLUS will place additional demands on the supervisors. Many PLUS programs call for major legislation, which requires public hearings and consultation with advisory bodies. In other words, the board will have to become more responsive to residents in order to fulfill its commitment under the new system.

These actual and projected aspects of board activity intensify a dilemma that the governing body faces: the need to choose between efficiency and responsiveness. Efficiency and responsiveness can be achieved simultaneously to a limited extent. For instance, if the supervisors can become better informed about matters covered in board meetings, they will be able to have shorter discussions and make prompter decisions. By promoting more efficient action, this improvement would permit the board to spend the conserved time on other business and perhaps be more responsive.

However, beyond a certain point, efficiency and responsiveness are mutually exclusive and demand a trade-off. Some of one quality must be sacrificed to gain more of the other. Public hearings illustrate this inverse relationship. If the supervisors reduce the time allotted for public hearings, they may become more efficient, since they will be able to devote additional attention to other issues. However, their responsiveness is measured partly by the time they spend in public hearings. Thus any limitation they impose on public hearings makes them seem less responsive. The dilemma involving efficiency and responsiveness confronts all governments, since they serve special interests in the course of performing prescribed duties.

There are many aspects of political behavior that could serve as measures for evaluating the activities of the board. Efficiency and responsiveness were selected for a number of reasons. First, they are broad qualities that encompass a variety of governmental functions. Secondly, they are universal traits that permit generalization about not only the Fairfax County government but also governance in other political subdivisions. Finally, they are of special significance to Fairfax County. This locality is undergoing a transition that began in the early 1950s and gained momentum in the last five years. To accommodate suburbanization, the bureaucracy has grown larger, more impersonal, and increasingly specialized and technical. Not only is the tension between responsiveness and efficiency apparent and pervasive, it is also complicated by the relationship between the Board of Supervisors and the county executive.

For purposes of analysis, efficiency and responsiveness can be conceived as two extremes on a continuum of orientation within the political system. Efficiency connotes rationality, concern with assignments and programs, impartiality, and emphasis on professional expertise. It is personified by the management analyst working under a planning, programming, and budgeting system. On the other hand, responsiveness implies a heuristic outlook, concern with individuals and their needs, favoritism, and the importance of personal connections. The big city boss of the old Democratic machine epitomizes this orientation. Most conventional politicians and bureaucrats would be located somewhere in the middle of this continuum, rather than at one of the ends. Nonetheless, the behavior of the Fairfax supervisors and county executive support the contention that political leaders tend toward responsiveness, whereas administrative chiefs are inclined toward efficiency in governmental operations.

A brief description of the Fairfax County government will provide a useful background for assessing the dynamics of board/staff interaction. The county government consists of elected officials, career civil service staff, and officials appointed by the Board of Supervisors and other governmental entities. The Board of Supervisors, commonwealth's attorney, clerk, and sheriff are elected by local voters. The board has the authority to appoint the county executive, deputy county executive, and agency chiefs.[56] Under normal circumstances, incumbents retain their positions. These officials head the departments and offices that comprise the core bureaucracy. This administrative staff is technically responsible to the board, but in practice the civil service system insulates most career bureaucrats from the elected supervisors.

No definitive criteria differentiates departments from offices, although most departments are "line" agencies and offices are "staff" agencies. Sometimes a new agency that partly or entirely supplants an existing agency is designated as an office. This procedure may soften the impact of the functional and structural change and ease the transition from the old to the new organization. For example, the Planning Division was reorganized in mid-1973 by establishing the Office of Comprehensive Planning (OCP). The office was semantically separate, but substantively undistinguishable from the Planning Division. This was a temporary arrangement that lasted about four months. The identity between OCP and Planning was formalized by the demotion of one senior official in the old Division of Planning.

Fairfax's judicial system is controlled by the general assembly, which appoints judges to the local courts. One of these, the circuit court, fills vacancies on the Electoral Board and the Board of Zoning Appeals (BZA). With the exception of these boards, the supervisors have sole authority to establish advisory bodies whose composition may include staff members, professionals, citizens, and supervisors. When vacancies occur, they also select representatives to serve on existing authorities, boards, commissions, councils, committees, and task forces. Presently, there are roughly seventy-five such advisory bodies in Fairfax County.[57] Unlike the administrative agencies, these advisory bodies are not accountable to the county executive, but report directly to the Board of Supervisors.

Although the supervisors appoint the county executive, the board and its chief administrative officer are also rivals. Their rivalry stems from the broad responsibility exercised by the board and the differing constituencies of the board and the county executive. The general assembly vested ultimate executive, legislative, and administrative authority in the Board of Supervisors. State enabling acts also required the urban county executive form to include specified departments. But the board determines the extent to which it participates in agency decisionmaking. The present supervisors have kept a tight rein on their administrative staff and have thereby restricted the power of the county executive. Their deep involvement in general county affairs exacerbates the inevitable competition between politician and bureaucrat.

The combined policymaking and administrative duties in the role of county supervisor reflect Fairfax's transition from rural to suburban jurisdiction that accelerated during the late 1950s and early 1960s. This dichotomous role encapsulates the tension between responsiveness and efficiency and thus is a microcosm of the strain that affects the entire government. It indicates a lack of theoretical understanding of this conflict. The supervisors must resolve this internal dilemma in their position in order to interact decisively with their administrative staffs.

The board and the county executive owe their primary allegiance to disparate groups. Fundamentally, the board is accountable to the electorate, while the county executive is accountable to the bureaucracy. Of course they need each other's assistance as well as the support of each other's principal constituents. But they apply the predictable priorities of politicians and bureaucrats in ranking the goals of efficiency and responsiveness. In relative terms, the board places responsiveness to citizens above efficient operations, whereas the county executive reverses the order.

Because the supervisors have declined to give the county executive substantial administrative autonomy, they must obstruct each other's overlapping operations to promote their conflicting priorities. One endemic form of obstruction heavily affects the conduct of county government: board reliance on advisory bodies rather than administrative staff. To understand this blocking device and place it in proper perspective, the context within which it occurs must be delineated. Therefore, the general purpose and operation of board meetings as well as the special use of advisory bodies by the board will be presented.

The weekly board meeting is the official forum for collective action by the supervisors including their interaction with the administrative staff. These sessions encapsulate the combined executive, legislative, and administrative powers of the board and the countywide and district demands that it must weigh. They also pinpoint the interdependence between board and staff. Usually the board provides direction and authorization for staff programs, while staff furnishes background information essential for board decisionmaking. But in addition to these shared efforts, each branch has separate and contradictory aims. The supervisors emphasize the political significance of the meeting, whereas staff members concentrate on its bureaucratic purpose. Board handling of issues therefore differs from the way that staff would want to proceed.

The crux of the problem is that board meetings are open to the public and receive local press coverage. Naturally, the supervisors take advantage of citizen and media attendance to improve their political standing. Not only do they gear their discussion to the audience, but they also encourage citizen participation by holding important public hearings in the evenings to maximize turnout. In contrast, many staff members who regularly attend these sessions consider citizen input as more of an impediment than an opportunity. Public scrutiny and involvement thus compounds the conflict between the supervisors' political priorities and their administrative staff's bureaucratic business.

In part, this heightened tension has led the county executive's staff, whose primary function is to assist the board, to curtail their cooperativeness. This response may not be deliberately intended to promote staff efficiency at the expense of board responsiveness, but it has that effect. Furthermore, the county administrative staff should not be viewed as a homogeneous unit, but rather as a collection of individuals and agencies that have varying goals and tasks. Thus some segments of the bureaucracy might be more favorably inclined toward the board's approach than others. However, the opinion that a desire to obstruct board effectiveness influences staff preparation for board meetings emerged in discussions with various participants in and observers of Fairfax County government.

The Advisory Bodies and Their Impact
on County Government

With respect to board meetings, the county executive's staff is an intermediary between the supervisors and administrative agencies. Sometimes this intermediary role produces a channel, and at other times a barrier to information flow and policy implementation. The supervisors, however, possess another public resource that they can deal with directly and have turned to with increasing frequency: the advisory bodies. Advisory bodies have become so numerous and, in some instances, powerful that they constitute a virtual counterbureaucracy. Like board meetings, the handling of these entities can promote or hinder governmental efficiency and responsiveness.

Assessment of the advisory bodies will encompass the following four steps. First, the different types of advisory bodies, their characteristics, and activities will be reviewed. Secondly, recent trends in the formation of these entities will be analyzed. Thirdly, possible causes and effects of their increased utilization will be explored. Finally, recommendations will be made to maximize the benefits and minimize the drawbacks inherent in the present arrangement.

Advisory bodies are established by the Board of Supervisors, either acting alone or in concert with other localities. Except for the Electoral Board and the BZA, which are controlled by the circuit court, all county advisory bodies are directly responsible to the supervisors. There are six basic types of advisory bodies: boards, authorities, commissions, councils, committees, and task forces (study groups, etc.).

Most boards, authorities, and commissions have statutory authorization. In other words, enabling legislation enacted by the federal government or the state of Virginia, or both, permits or requires the establishments of these entities. Both boards and commissions may perform quasi-judicial functions, although boards often have additional responsibilities, such as magisterial and representative. Authorities are usually delegated functionary and administrative capabilities.

Councils are generally deliberative bodies whose primary role is to collect and disseminate information and generate policy proposals. In contrast to authorities, they do not ordinarily perform specific assigned functions in the community-at-large. Councils have a broader mandate than committees and task forces, and many are interjurisdictional.

Committees and task forces are not generally statutory, have a more limited purpose than the other bodies, and are often temporary. They are frequently created to study a specific topic and submit a report summarizing their findings and suggestions.

Membership on advisory bodies includes supervisors, administrative staff members, professionals or experts, citizens, and members of other advisory bodies. The composition of advisory bodies may be drawn from representatives of one or more of these groups. Most of the advisory bodies that the supervisors have established on their own initiative contain a cross section of two or more groups.

As of November 1973, there were seventy-five advisory bodies in Fairfax County: twenty-four boards, seven authorities, fourteen commissions, seven councils, fifteen committees, and eight task forces. Table 4-1 lists the advisory bodies and, in most cases, provides dates of establishment and composition of membership. As Table 4-1 indicates, the ranks of these entities have multiplied since 1964, and the strongest surge has occurred under the present Board of Supervisors. Of the seventy advisory bodies for which creation dates were available, eleven were in existence before 1964, eight were established between 1964 and 1967, twenty-four between 1968 and 1971, and twenty-seven since 1972. In other words, 32 percent were formed by the preceding supervisors and 36 percent by the current supervisors less than half-way through their term. The advisory bodies that the current board created will be explored in greater depth.

Of the twenty-seven advisory bodies that the supervisors established in 1972 and 1973, twenty-two of these represented Fairfax County alone and five included other jurisdictions in the Washington metropolitan area. Only two had statutory authorization; the other twenty-five originated from the independent initiative of the board and other local governments. The emphasis was on committees, and twelve of these most recently constituted advisory bodies are of this type. Of the remaining fifteen, there are four boards, six task forces, three commissions, and two councils. The membership of all but three commissions was ascertained. Nineteen or 70 percent included citizens, and seven, or nearly 25 percent of the total, drew all of their members from the citizenry.[58]

Trends of accelerated formation of advisory bodies and substantial citizen involvement emerge from the above statistics. The advisory bodies were created under different circumstances to meet a variety of needs. However, two general conditions, one local and the other nationwide, also appear to have influenced recent formation: rivalry between the board and administrative staff and pressure for citizen participation. Characteristics of the newest entities suggest that inadequate staff support and the demand for public involvement contributed to increased board reliance on the counterbureaucracy. On the surface, this approach solves these two problems facing the supervisors. In the continual conflict between efficiency and responsiveness, they are able to preempt the county executive, since the advisory bodies are accountable to them alone.

Normally, the board submits a request or assigns a project to the administrative staff by working through the Office of the County Executive. But when the county executive carries out a board order or delegates it to an agency, he can impose his orientation in a number of ways. First he can expedite or delay completion of the project depending on the priority he assigns it. Secondly, he

Table 4-1
Fairfax County Advisory Bodies: November 1973

Type of Advisory Body	Statutory Authorization	Year Formed	Membership
BOARDS			
Air Pollution Control	yes	1967	citizens
Architectural Review	yes	1968	professionals
Building Code and Appeals	yes	1954	staff and professionals
Crossroads Advisory	no	1973	staff, citizens
Electrical Review	yes	1922	professionals
Equalization of Real Estate Assessments	yes	1968	professionals, citizens
Fairfax-Falls Church Community Mental Health & Mental Retardation Services*	yes	1969	professionals, citizens
Fairfax House Advisory	no	1963	Not Available (N.A.)
Fair Housing	yes	1968	citizens
Health Care Advisory	no	1973	citizens (district and at-large representatives), professionals
Housing Hygiene	yes	1965	citizens
Library	yes	1939	citizens, (district and at-large representatives), professionals
License Review	yes	1970	staff, citizens
Northern Virginia Community College*	yes	1965	N.A.

Table 4-1 (cont.)

Type of Advisory Body	Statutory Authorization	Year Formed	Membership
Plumbing Examiners & Appeals	no	1969	professionals
Policemen's Pension & Retirement	yes	1941	staff
Restoration	no	1972	staff, citizen groups
Road Viewers	yes	1969	citizens (district and at-large representatives)
School	yes	N.A.	citizens (district and at-large representatives)
Social Services	yes	1969	staff, citizens
Stream Valley	no	1973	staff, citizens
Fairfax Community Action Program	yes	1965	citizens
COMMISSIONS			
Anti-Poverty	no	1972	citizen groups
Civil Service	yes	1957	citizens
On Aging	no	1973	citizens (district and at-large representatives)
On Women	no	1971	citizens (district and at-large representatives)
Consumer Protection & Public Utilities	no	1964	citizens
Fire	yes	1970	professionals, citizens
Highway Safety	yes	1968	supervisors, citizens

History	yes	1969	professionals
Northern Virginia Planning District*	yes	1969	supervisors, citizens
Northern Virginia Regional Juvenile Detention Home*	no	1956	staff, citizens
Northern Virginia Transportation	no	1964	supervisors
Planning	yes	1938	citizens (district and at-large representatives)
Tree	no	1973	staff, citizens
Tenant-Landlord	yes	1971	citizens
COUNCILS			
Northern Virginia Comprehensive Health Planning	no	1970	citizens
Environmental Quality Advisory	yes	1972	citizens (district and at-large representatives)
Fairfax County Criminal Justice Coordinating	no	1971	citizens, citizen groups
Northern Virginia Criminal Justice Advisory*	yes	1970	staff, citizens
Environmental Research Advisory*	no	1972	citizens
Of Governments*	yes	1957	supervisors
Of Arts	no	1966	N.A.
COMMITTEES			
Bicentennial	N.A.	1971	citizens
Council of Governments Advisory*	no	1973	citizens

Table 4-1 (cont.)

Type of Advisory Body	Statutory Authorization	Year Formed	Membership
Dulles Industrial Development Planning	no	1972	staff, citizen groups, citizens
Engineering Standards Review	yes	1973	professionals, citizens, staff
Fairfax County Governmental Study	no	1972	citizens
Gas Line Safety	no	1973	supervisors, professionals
I-95 Center Policy	no	1973	staff, citizens
Legislative	no	1973	N.A.
Park and County Financial	no	1972	staff, professionals
Police Community Relations	no	1972	staff, citizens, citizen groups
Site Selection	no	1968	N.A.
Solid Waste Disposal Planning	no	1972	staff, supervisors, professionals, citizens
Temporary Housing Settlement Review	no	1972	N.A.
Transit Corridor	no	1973	N.A.
Zoning Ordinance Study	no	1970	staff, professionals, citizens
AUTHORITIES			
Economic Development	yes	1964	professionals, citizens
Northern Virginia Regional Park*	yes	1959	N.A.

Park	1950	yes	citizens
Redevelopment & Housing	1965	yes	citizens
Upper Occoquan Sewage	1971	yes	citizens
Water	1957	yes	citizens
Washington Metropolitan Area Transit*	N.A.	yes	supervisors
TASK FORCES, ETC.			
Fairfax Hospital Association Board of Trustees	1973	no	supervisors, citizens
Human Services Task Force	1973	no	staff
Joint Task Force on Housing	1970	no	N.A.
N.V.P.D.C. Occoquan Study Group*	1972	no	supervisors, staff, citizens, (district, at-large)
N.V.P.D.C. Regional Task Force for Gerontological Planning*	1972	no	citizens
Supplemental Retirement System Board of Trustees	1955	yes	staff, citizens
Task Force on Comprehensive Planning and Land Use Control	1973	no	staff, supervisors

*Interjurisdictional

Source: Office of the Chairman of the Board, "Fairfax County Boards, Authorities Commissions, etc., Appointed by the Board of Supervisors" (Fairfax County, November 1, 1973).

can interpret the request to reflect his or other staff members' assessment of the critical issues. Thirdly, he can attempt to carry out the assignment impartially but receive biased results from agency staff.

Reliance on advisory bodies increases board control over designated studies or operations by eliminating the middleman role of the county executive. Often agency employees are assigned part-time or new employees are hired to staff offices of the more permanent advisory bodies. For instance, the Fairfax Redevelopment and Housing Authority has an executive director and several support staff members, and the Planning Commission has an administrative assistant and several secretaries. Board members can communicate directly with both assigned staff and appointed members of advisory bodies. Thus they can avoid potential interference from the county executive by working around him and dealing with the counterbureaucracy.

At the same time they by-pass the county executive, the supervisors expand their responsiveness by stressing citizen representation on advisory bodies. Limiting the county executive's involvement in board proposals prevents the possible imposition of staff's more efficiency-oriented objectives. In contrast, the supervisors make a positive effort to increase their responsiveness when they rely on the counterbureaucracy with its citizen members. An invitation for county residents to attend meetings, perform research, and compile recommendations is a responsive action. Advisory bodies that include residents promote the expression of their opinions and thus their contribution to local government.

However, the supervisors seem no less anxious to defer to residents' bias than to the county executive's. A desire to retain maximum command over county administration would partly explain their preference for committees and task forces. By focusing on these more limited and temporary advisory bodies, rather than on the more powerful boards, authorities, and commissions, they offer a weaker role to citizens.

On the other hand, their concentration on committees and task forces may stem from a commitment to local independence. Many of the other advisory bodies require statutory authorization, which would have precluded spontaneous board action. Furthermore, the actual impact of these bodies is more important than their nominal features. Board intentions must be gauged by the responsibility delegated to these committees and task forces and by the attention that is paid to their findings. Since many of these advisory bodies have been in existence for only a year, it is too early to evaluate board utilization of them.

Although many new advisory bodies have not produced tangible accomplishments, the general effects of the counterbureaucracy are evident. First, greater board reliance on advisory bodies has compounded administrative fragmentation, both within the counterbureaucracy and between it and the bureaucracy. County environmental protection activities illustrate the resulting multiplication of entities and compartmentalization of functions.

Since they took office, the current supervisors have established the Office of Environmental Affairs (OEA), Environmental Quality Advisory Council (EQAC), Tree Commission, Restoration Board, Stream Valley Board, and Environmental Research Advisory Council (in conjunction with the other jurisdictions represented on the Northern Virginia Planning District Commission).[59] This list omits environment-related areas, such as solid waste disposal, industrial development, planning and land use, and transportation. Some county agencies, citizen organizations, and advisory bodies are represented on several of these environmental entities. In certain instances, their operations coincide. The OEA, for example, essentially serves as the staff to the EQAC. More often, however, no formal relationships exist among these entities, which increases the likelihood that they will pursue common projects separately or assume inconsistent positions on issues.

Secondly, because advisory bodies are functionally independent of the bureaucracy, their staff or appointed members may disrupt routine governmental operations. Due to a lack of information or a refusal to follow established procedures, they may fail to provide necessary cooperation. The OCP has encountered both of these obstacles in collecting data for the capital improvements program.

All governmental entities were sent forms that would permit planning staff evaluation of their needs for capital facilities. Several advisory bodies balked at this procedure, because they did not understand or accept it. In one case, a staff member contacted the Office of the County Executive to verify the procedure's propriety. This move was counterproductive, since the OCP operation was authorized, and the staff member only delayed its completion.

Finally, although the advisory bodies have basic functional autonomy, they can exaggerate their independence to their disadvantage. Advisory bodies that are insulated from bureaucratic intervention may become isolated from administrative support. For instance, they are all financially accountable to the county executive, since their budgets are reviewed by his staff. Communication gaps can originate at either end, and uncooperative advisory bodies may stimulate the same behavior they display in budgeting and other administrative personnel. Thus lack of coordination between administrative agencies and advisory bodies hinders bureaucratic efficiency and counterbureaucratic responsiveness.

The trend of increasing board reliance on advisory bodies is likely to continue. Even if board/staff relations improve and measures that further efficiency and responsiveness are instituted, pressure for citizen participation will undoubtedly persist. Since neither elected officials nor bureaucrats favor establishing a sub-local level of government, advisory bodies will remain the major vehicle for community involvement in county affairs. Therefore, alternatives to the present conditions should concentrate on improving and strengthening the present structure, rather than by-passing or dismantling it. To mitigate governmental fragmentation and lack of coordination, the following personnel, organizational, and procedural modifications are recommended.

Recommendations

Advisory Body Liaison Staff. An advisory body liaison staff should be established under the chairman of the Board of Supervisors. This staff should be directly responsible to the board and therefore should work out of the chairman's office rather than the county executive's office. Since the county executive's staff will continue to provide assistance to the board, the liaison staff will have to coordinate their activities with them. One member of the county executive's staff should be designated as the main contact to ensure clear communication. The primary role of the liaison staff, however, will be to monitor the activities of the advisory bodies. This task should be simplified by several other proposals.

Umbrella Organizations. Umbrella organizations, composed of representatives of functionally related advisory bodies, should also be formed. This superstructure should include all entities created and staffed exclusively by the supervisors. Advisory bodies established by referendum or interjurisdictional action, and those whose members are appointed by other public officials should be omitted, because the supervisors lack substantial control over them.

The number of umbrella organizations should be small enough to avoid fragmentation on this higher level, yet large enough to afford differentiation of activities. These steering committees should represent the full range of advisory bodies, although their scope will depend on the specific functional areas they address. Several possible categories are environmental protection, construction and engineering, and transportation. In the course of setting up this superstructure, the liaison staff and other staff members may propose consolidation of some advisory bodies. The reorganization could reveal duplication of functions and overlapping jurisdictions that could be eliminated most effectively by merging two or more entities. Thus, major and minor structural alterations may be required to improve operations.

Communication. The existence and activities of advisory bodies should be more widely publicized. At present, a list of all boards, commissions, committees, councils, authorities, and task forces, compiled by the Office of the Chairman of the Board, is available primarily to county officials. This list gives the title, membership, and purpose of most advisory bodies. It should be circulated to citizens and private organizations and expanded to reflect procedural modifications detailed below.

All advisory bodies and steering committees should provide schedules of their meetings and other activities, such as field trips, to the liaison staff. They should also submit progress reports, which would be forwarded to the board and county executive. In the case of individual advisory bodies, monthly reports should be prepared, which summarize current studies and operations. Umbrella organizations, with their coordinating rather than investigative function, would submit quarterly memoranda on their activities.

The liaison staff should keep the public, as well as the board and administrative staff, informed about the counterbureaucracy. Since advisory bodies are the primary vehicle for citizen participation, the county has a special obligation to appraise residents of their role. Accordingly, copies of meeting schedules should be distributed to the local media and posted in county office buildings. Public attendance and testimony at advisory body sessions can be encouraged in this way.

Conclusion

Thus the proposals for improving the contents of board meetings and the functioning of advisory bodies concentrate on cooperation and communication. Both of these major arenas for local government are presently plagued by deliberate and accidental forms of counterproductivity. Apart from the tension involving responsiveness and efficiency, the growing size and complexity of the county administrative apparatus increases the likelihood of uncoordinated and inconsistent action. Some duplication and waste is inevitable and perhaps desirable in that perfect congruence can only be achieved in a rigid and stagnant environment. But mitigation of the defects that thwart efficiency and responsiveness can only benefit the county government and citizens.

5

The Board's Initial Efforts to Regulate Development: January 1972-February 1973

Introduction

The present board rejected their predecessors' relatively passive approach to land use regulation. While it was necessary to ferret out the policies of previous boards, explicit policymaking is a hallmark of the current supervisors. But whereas their predecessors were too cautious by contemporary standards, the present supervisors were decidedly overzealous in their first steps to bring about change. Ironically, their vigorous pursuit of a new strategy generated equally vigorous opposition that made them retreat to some earlier practices that they had maligned. When confronted with judicial repudiation of their stringent measures, they resorted to traditional controls that were less drastic and more acceptable.

Piecemeal action and an emphasis on policy formulation characterized the board's first year in office. It was committed to limiting local growth and evidently felt that issuing policies was the most decisive and expedient move that it could make on its own. In order to achieve its objective, the board had to wrest policymaking responsibility from the county executive, George C. Kelley, and the housing industry. The board's preoccupation with policymaking produced a three-way conflict involving these participants in the local political arena.

In retrospect, the supervisors might have been better off if they had not won such resounding victories in the general election of 1971 and the special election of 1972. Apparently the electoral mandate to expand public regulation of growth caused them to don only half of the leadership mantle: they demonstrated an ability to act but not to inspire. For over a year, they governed the county like military commanders rather than political representatives. They launched both a public relations and legislative assault on the opposition, which was entrenched outside and inside the local administration. Their strategy brought only partial victory, however, because they underestimated their vulnerability on several fronts. They supplanted the county executive, but only temporarily confounded the housing industry, which retaliated with a successful defense. The supervisors not only antagonized property owners and developers, but also alienated former officials and the county media and confused their administrative staff. Finally, the economics of housing in the metropolitan area produced adverse repercussions for Fairfax residents that triggered a citizen backlash aimed at the board.

49

At the beginning of their term, the supervisors confronted three different sets of expectations concerning growth control held by citizens, developers, and George Kelley. To fulfill their election pledge to limit development, they challenged the housing industry, which wanted market forces to determine growth rates, and the county executive, who wanted to promote growth on a least-cost basis.

The supervisors were more forceful in their treatment of developers than in their dealings with George Kelley. Two factors account for their low-keyed manner toward the county executive. First, the new board members had to gain experience, establish contacts with key interest groups, and learn to work together before they could confront his domineering personality and tight rein on the county administration. Secondly, the board and the county executive agreed on growth policy up to a point, and they were initially able to overlook some differences. The events surrounding Kelley's resignation suggest that for him the struggle for ultimate authority took precedence over the clash in policy orientation.

The board dealt with the housing industry and the county executive simultaneously by adopting policies that promoted its aims. The contents of these policies affected developers, since they represented expanded public regulation at the expense of private property rights. Their impact on Kelley involved procedure as well as substance. He favored increased governmental intervention, but espoused a more permissive philosophy of development and resented board initiative in land use control.

Four major decisions illustrate the board's policymaking style and antagonistic attitude toward developers during the first year of its term: imposition of a rezoning moratorium, introduction of an ordinance curtailing the use of septic tanks, refusal to allocate available capacity in sewage treatment plants, and administrative harassment. After analyzing these measures and the reactions they elicited, other aspects of board administration and trends in population and housing since 1972 will be discussed.

The Rezoning Moratorium

Contending that existing county district plans were inadequate, the board declared a moratorium on all rezoning cases in order to allow staff preparation of a new countywide master plan. Its sharp criticism of earlier plans irked former officials, who resented the new members' attitude that they were going to undertake the county's first real planning effort. While former public servants were miffed, the housing industry was distraught. In the words of one industry spokesman, the board wanted to "cut off their break and water." The moratorium was to last six to twelve months, a delay that would have wreaked havoc with the development process because of the lead time required to set the various stages of production in motion. Notwithstanding this measure, county rezoning operations were chaotic. One case had been deferred for seven years, and newer cases were being processed before older ones.[60]

The moratorium combined with this administrative disarray prompted a number of developers to file suit against the board. Twelve plaintiffs consolidated their cases into one case, *DeLuca Enterprises Inc. v. the Board of County Supervisors of Fairfax County, Virginia.* They all basically claimed that the moratorium was a violation of due process. Filed in March 1972, the suit never received a final disposition. The circuit court ordered the supervisors to continue hearing rezoning applications, and they complied.[61] They established a zoning docket and reserved the last meeting of each month for rezoning cases until late in 1973.

Allocation of Sewage Treatment Capacity

The board intended to slow the pace of current development as well as future construction. Because most new housing utilizes county sewage treatment facilities, the board attempted to stall projects that were in progress by withholding sewer hook-ups. It instituted a time-phasing procedure that curtailed distribution of available capacity at the Blue Plains treatment plant. This policy, adopted in late 1972, produced another rash of industry lawsuits and a judicial rebuff of the board. In *Feldman et al.*, the circuit court ruled that the supervisors could not deny sewer hook-ups if excess capacity and a demand for that capacity existed.[62]

The tenuousness of trying to control growth by limiting use of available sewage treatment facilities was even acknowledged by county staff. The county executive's *Five-Year Countywide Development Program* pointed out that by the time procedures preliminary to construction, such as site plan or subdivision plot review, were underway, "the County had been involved in decisions which tended to set a precedent for development."[63] It could not legitimately renege on this automatic commitment.

The supervisors were more successful in denying sewer hook-ups to the overloaded Lower Potomac treatment plan. In this instance, the issue was water pollution, rather than slower growth, and the circuit court found the board policy justifiable.[64] This measure was of limited value, however, because it only dealt with a symptom and not the disease of growth that outstripped county services. Furthermore, its utility was threatened by the conditions that fostered the ban. The Virginia State Water Control Board insisted in mid-1973, around the same time when the favorable court ruling was handed down, that the county meet its water pollution standards. Raising the quality of the effluent necessitated improvements in the plant that would expand its capacity and thus permit more sewer hook-ups and development.[65]

Ironically, the board's lack of alternative leverage points in the development process forced it to revert to the deterministic policy of land use control by sewer construction practiced by its predecessors. This technique, which the current supervisors initially rejected as part of an inadequate regulatory system, was at least viable under appropriate circumstances.

Restrictions on the Use of Septic Tanks

Board efforts to withhold sewage treatment services for new housing caused delays and lawsuits that were costly to developers. To circumvent the county facilities, some builders opted for residential construction using septic tanks. This alternative was only a partial solution, however, because it is relatively impractical and very expensive. Nonetheless, board denial of sewer hook-ups and resistance to expand existing plants generated a flood of applications for septic tank permits.

In an attempt to close this development loophole, the board proposed two amendments to the ordinance governing the use of septic tanks. First, it moved to increase the minimum lot size for a dwelling on septic from one-half to one acre. Secondly, it proposed a prohibition on pumping waste for septic tank disposal. The former restriction would have made construction prohibitively expensive, while the latter would have severely limited the locations eligible for septic tanks.

The obvious intent of these amendments was to curtail growth rather than promote the general welfare since the capacity to accommodate septic tanks on half-acre lots and the need for pumping sewage are both widespread in the county. Thus the validity of the board's policy was at best dubious. A court challenge would have probably yielded a ruling against the supervisors, and industry opposition to these amendments was so strenuous that lawsuits were assured. The imminent threat of another legal defeat convinced the supervisors to relent, and neither of the amendments was approved.[66]

Administrative Harassment of Developers

As the rezoning moratorium, time-phased allocation of sewer hook-ups, and restrictions on the use of septic tanks indicate, the board's instrument of policymaking was severely blunted on the judicial front. To reinforce this policy broadside, the board engaged in sniping on the administrative front. Utilizing the case-by-case review practiced by their predecessors. the supervisors harassed developers that they could not vanquish.

With their strategy stymied by court challenges, the supervisors applied tactics of delay. On the one hand, they postponed verdicts on rezoning applications. Even though they were under court order to hear cases, they could defer final decisions for weeks or months after the public hearing by demanding additional information. On the other hand, they multiplied the steps that both developers and administrative staff had to take in the development procedure. There were more forms for the applicants to fill out and more reviews of construction programs by the processors than under previous boards. Development became an ordeal of trial by paper.

One victim of this foot dragging treatment was Reston. Its case is particularly striking because of past county dealings with the new town and its significance as a viable alternative to suburban sprawl.

At its inception, Reston enjoyed a special status in Fairfax County. It received preferential treatment from the board and land use regulatory agencies because of its commitment to planned growth. A self-sufficient and integrated living and working environment was its goal, and the board that served from 1960 to 1964 welcomed Reston as a solution to suburban sprawl. But the new town gradually lost its privileged position as later boards apparently rejected the independence and momentum inherent in its development.

In 1962 Reston's developers prepared and obtained county approval for a master plan of development required under its RPC zoning classification. Periodic review of the development program, stipulated in the zoning ordinance, should have substituted for the usual rezoning application process. But for the last nine years, the planned community has had to request rezonings of each piece of property scheduled for development.

The present supervisors imposed tighter restrictions and longer delays than their predecessors, and jeopardized the new town's future. During their first year in office, they treated Reston as if it were a conventional subdivision that would destroy the landscape and burden the county with additional demands for public facilities to serve new residents. It apparently disregarded Reston's earlier contribution to environmental protection and ongoing commitment to balanced growth. The storm drainage provisions of the county zoning ordinance were modeled after the standards contained in Reston's development program. Also, the new town's master plan included public services, which the county had to install in conventionally subdivided neighborhoods.

On an average of three times each week, the county applied foot dragging techniques that blocked or delayed some aspect of development. Adherence to Reston's master plan, predicated on three to five years lead time for engineering and design, was essential for continued construction.[67] Board tactics rendered the development program increasingly inoperative to the point where advance planning became financial folly. The supervisors eventually drove the Gulf Corporation to contemplate withdrawal of its investment in the new town. They continued to harass Reston in 1973, but the pattern was set during their first year in office. For this reason, this characterization of their tactics applies primarily to 1972.

Conflict between the Board and
County Executive

The board's power base had been eroded by the county executive as well as by the housing industry. During its first year in office, the board was attempting to outmaneuver both developers and George C. Kelley, Jr. County government was under Kelley's thumb because of administrative changes he had engineered. The board had to wrest decisionmaking authority from him in order to pursue its goals, especially in the area of growth control.

Whereas judicial precedents had hindered the supervisors in their campaign against the housing industry, legislative stipulations gave them an advantage over Kelley. The Virginia state code delegated ultimate local authority to the governing body, which could redistribute various functions at will. Thus while their predecessors deferred to Kelley's administrative judgment, the present supervisors chose to assert their executive prerogative. The county executive had no legal recourse because the board's effort was entirely justified. Kelley could only attempt to thwart the board. He tried and failed.

Perhaps because they stood on firm legal ground and shared some growth control tactics with Kelley, the supervisors' manner toward him was cautious. And while their heavy-handed dealings with developers usually yielded negative results, their even-tempered handling of Kelley proved successful. The county executive resigned after a supervisor criticized him publicly. This move was apparently not calculated to force Kelley's departure, but it exposed the unbreachable gap between the board and county executive.

The board unintentionally provoked Kelley's resignation over the issue of decisionmaking in the area of sewage treatment facilities. One member accused him of concealing a report on the capacity at a plant that would have influenced board action. Kelley denied deliberately withholding the information and resigned over this lack of trust.[68] Although the accusation was not made to precipitate Kelley's resignation, it achieved this result because the board's views on development and concentration of policymaking authority had evidently grown too far apart from the county executive's to permit compromise and reconciliation.

It is important to review the salient aspects of George C. Kelley's growth policy, since it is woven into the administrative fabric he bequeathed the board. Some of the difficulties encountered in implementing PLUS stem from the incongruence between the board's objectives and the objectives that Kelley's governmental structure was designed to achieve.

As county executive, Kelley directed the preparation of a five-year county-wide development program, which delineated his philosophy of suburbanization. Recognizing the previous paucity of growth policy, he sought to impose his views on the local government. The fundamental premise of his program was that:

Growth in certain areas of Fairfax County would be less expensive than in other areas during the next five years, because some areas had excess public facility capacities and the capital costs required to absorb new growth would be minimal.[69]

He proposed to analyze alternative growth levels in order to arrive at a least-cost growth rate that would guide development from 1972 to 1977.

Kelley was determined to eliminate leap-frogging development that had occurred particularly in the 1960s when cost of land close to urbanized areas rose sharply and highway construction facilitated commuting from more remote parts of the county. The extent of this scattered suburbanization is illustrated by the fact that all residential construction between 1960 and 1970 could have been accommodated on land inside the Capital beltway. Actually, of the more than 65,000 new housing units built during the decade, roughly 18,500 were located in the eastern, 27,000 in the central, and 19,600 in the western portions of the county.[70] Thus about twenty-eight percent of the residential growth occurred where all of it could have fit.

Complementing the cost component of Kelley's growth policy was a revenue component. His revenue strategy was detailed in the financial plan that was the companion volume to the development plan. There were three major conclusions of the financial analysis. First, a revenue gap would exist over the five-year period because expenditures would exceed receipts. Secondly, the revenue gap would be greater for the lower population projections than for higher projections. Thirdly, the bond market would limit the 1977 county population to 613,900 persons,[71] which was 113,900 more than the 1 January 1972 population of approximately 503,000. Thus to achieve what he considered an optimal five-year growth rate, Kelley wanted the county to grow as much as facilities and financing would permit. He proposed to maximize utilization of excess capacity in existing public facilities and minimize the anticipated financial deficit that the county would experience.

Kelley's least-cost analysis contains two major flaws, which cast doubt on the validity of his conclusions. First, the analysis only deals with the short-run situation. Ordinarily, in the short run, capital investment raises the cost of government services substantially, and it is more economical to increase operating expenditures. Over the long term, however, total expenditures may prove that the capital investment was a necessary element of the least-cost solution.

Secondly, the topic of the study—cost-effectiveness for county public facilities—excludes all other costs of development, such as transportation and social services. It also ignores the benefit side of the equation, for instance the trade-off between pollution and environmental protection that comprehensive growth policy should address. Kelley's narrow perspective produced an incomplete assessment of the problem and an inadequate solution.

Thus in terms of its orientation toward growth as well as administration, the board was justified in precipitating Kelley's departure from Fairfax County government. The board followed up on this development five months later by appointing Kelley's deputy, Robert W. Wilson, as county executive. During the interim period, Wilson evidently showed a willingness to comply with the guidelines that the supervisors established for county governance.

Bureaucratic Repercussions of Board Actions

Although the board repudiated Kelley's growth strategy, it maintained most of the administrative machinery he forged. It reinstituted the single deputy county executive position and placed the Office of Management and Budget (OMB) beyond the county executive's immediate control. But for four months after Kelley's departure, the land use control system he created remained virtually intact.

The supervisors' battle with the builders and continuation of Kelley's agency structure confused the bureaucracy and consequently caused inefficiency. The adverse impact of these two actions was most pronounced in the operations of the Clerk to the board and the DCD, respectively.

The Clerk to the board maintains records of all official board activities. This office publishes ordinances and resolutions proposed by the supervisors and handles requests for testimony and other presentations at public hearings. Under normal conditions, the office's primary responsibilities are to make tape recordings of weekly board meetings, issue a rough unofficial summary of the discussion for staff use, and prepare official minutes summarizing the meetings several weeks later.

Routine operations ceased, however, when developers inundated the circuit court with lawsuits challenging the board's new regulatory measures. Each case required a written transcript of the applicable portions of board discussions that occurred during weekly sessions. The Clerk's office had to shift its priorities to verbatim transcripts of specific board meetings, which caused a six-month backlog for official minutes of all other meetings.

This backlog impeded normal communication between the board and administrative staff. Agencies that received projects assigned by the supervisors often referred to the official minutes if their representatives did not attend the particular session when the request was made. The context for many board proposals was therefore unavailable to officials in timely fashion. Consequently, some board requests did not receive a prompt and proper staff response due to incomplete background information. The result was inefficient government from the standpoint of not only the board and staff, but also citizens who wanted to obtain official minutes in order to follow board activities more closely.

It was contradictory rather than fragmentary instructions that left County

Development staff baffled. The DCD was charged with expediting private construction under Kelley's administrative reorganization. Agency staff had no authority to limit requests for site plan or subdivision plat approval and building or sewer permits. Its function was to ensure compliance with official standards governing private land use.

However, the board's attempt to limit growth by deferring rezoning decisions and withholding excess sewage capacity demanded comparable action by agency personnel. They were under pressure to perform their assigned duties inefficiently in order to stall instead of facilitate development. The agency was hardly prepared for this unlikely bureaucratic quandary, as demonstrated by its indecisive treatment of developers.

County Development's dilemma was exacerbated by an upsurge in demand for building permits in late 1972. Two official measures caused the rush, which one observer felt was so massive due to industry distrust of the board. First, the sewer availability charge, or fee assessed for each new hook-up to the sewer system, was raised from $600 to $1,000. News of the increase was leaked before board action was finalized. Developers thought that the new rate would apply to any project that had not received a building permit. Events proved the developers overly pessimistic, as it became apparent that any project under consideration by County Development staff before the cut-off date was subject to the lower charge.

Secondly, rumors that a sewer moratorium would be imposed in the southern part of the county served by the Pohick watershed also spurred developers to obtain building permits. By accelerating the design phase of projects and obtaining building permits, developers would have made a greater financial commitment. They hoped that this monetary investment would add weight to their requests for sewer hook-ups. The rumors were accurate, and the ban went into effect.[72]

In the meantime, County Development staff was caught in the middle and was pulled in opposite directions. On the one side was the board, which wanted it to slow down their operations, and on the other side, the industry, which wanted it to speed up procedures. The department issued the building permits, which amounted to a 25 percent increase over 1971,[73] as required by law. But industry representatives reported that staff members became evasive and hesitated to sign off on projects because they anticipated adverse board reaction. Only board denial of roughly 63 percent of the rezoning applications during 1972[74] alleviated some of the tension that the DCD felt.

Fallout from the supervisors' feud with the housing industry and with the county executive permeated the entire county government. But the consternation was particularly acute in the Office of the Clerk to the board and the DCD, two agencies caught in the crossfire. Another group that registered an intense reaction to the board's growth control activities was the general public.

Public Reaction to County Policies

The supervisors had predicated their offensive against the housing industry and county executive on public support for their land use control goals. However, this popular base gradually eroded as a result of socio-economic trends whose effects were glaring. Specifically, the county population and housing values rose at higher rates after the board took office than in the 1960s. The board's strong stand on development regulation invited blame, and a citizen backlash occurred in the form of public criticism of county policies. The actual causes of these trends are difficult to pinpoint since regional and national economics are involved. It is clear, nonetheless, that the board bore only part of the responsibility, even though it was the obvious target.

The major complaints raised by residents related to crowding and taxes. They resented new development that destroyed open space and brought more congestion to local highways. They also objected to their steadily increasing assessments. Three indicators—population growth, residential construction, and housing values—substantiate the claims of county citizens.

There were an estimated 563,800 residents of Fairfax County on 1 January 1974. From a 1 January population of roughly 503,000, 30,900 and 29,900 persons were added in 1972 and 1973 respectively.[75] Thus the county population grew at rates of 6.1 percent and 5.6 percent since the board had taken office, compared to an annual average of 5.3 percent or 24,000 persons for 1970 and 1971.

To accommodate these new inhabitants, the housing stock also expanded. From a total of 140,330 units at the end of 1971, 15,130 were added in 1972 and 9,940 in 1973.[76] This new supply was evidently inadequate to meet consumer demand. The average sale price of houses jumped from $43,500 in 1971 to $47,600 in 1972 and $53,000 by mid-1973.[77] This 22 percent rise in housing values was reflected in property taxes. Prices rose so fast that the county began assessing property annually in 1972, instead of every three years. As a result, some homeowners experienced reassessments of as much as 40 percent in two years.[78]

These trends in population, housing and taxes can be linked to five influences on supply and demand. First, employment in the Washington, D.C. area continued to expand in the early 1970s, which created consumer demand for housing. Secondly, the previous board had granted rezonings, and County Development staff had taken additional steps that committed the county to a substantial amount of growth. There were 13,579 building permits issued during 1971.[79] In the past, an eighteen month lag between permit issuance and completion had occurred. Therefore, many committed units were probably added to the housing stock in early 1973.[80]

Thirdly, pressure for even more growth in Fairfax was generated by the 1971 sewer moratorium that the Environmental Protection Agency imposed on

Montgomery and Prince George's Counties. The ban, still in effect, prohibited new construction in these Maryland suburbs until additional treatment facilities were provided. Developers turned to Fairfax County, the nearby jurisdiction with a large supply of vacant land. New construction was facilitated by the fourth influence, a drop in the interest rate. The tight money market of 1970 expanded over the following eighteen months. At the beginning of 1972, the prime rate was 5 percent. It was 6 percent in early 1973 and only began to climb steeply in June.[81]

Finally, the board adopted policies that inadvertently encouraged development. In particular, the 67 percent increase in the sewer availability charge and the sewer moratorium in the Pohick watershed caused developers to accelerate their projects as a hedge against the future. Ironically, the board's commitment to limited growth without effective controls precipitated a record of 16,943 building permits issued in 1972.[82]

Thus the supervisors were both the authors of their own fate and victims of circumstances beyond their authority. While they were perhaps the most apparent participants in local land use control, a variety of regional and national supply and demand forces set the stage for the boomerang effect of their policies. One reason county residents focused on the board's role was the publicity campaign that the housing industry initiated in the spring of 1973.

Board harassment of the housing industry generated an atmosphere of mutual distrust. Since the courtroom was the major forum for interaction during 1972, the parties became polarized as each tried to discredit the other. Board policies and therefore lawsuits tapered off in early 1973, but the antagonism and villification remained. The supervisors saw developers as rapists of the land, while the industry claimed the board wanted to quash the entrepreneurial spirit.[83] In this hostile climate, developers decided to take their case to the people and launched a public relations counterattack. Their campaign continued after PLUS was adopted, but had its strongest impact on the supervisors at its outset.

Developers used the phrase "no-growth policies" as both a defense and an offense. On the one hand, they contended that the board was denying them the right to make a living. On the other hand, they claimed that no new housing would be available for county residents. One especially touching poster showed a small boy holding a beagle puppy. The caption read: "If we can't get a house, can I still keep him?" Industry spokesmen knew they were exaggerating the effect of board policies since many had been overturned in court. But they felt they were accurately depicting the position of the majority of supervisors.

Thus as county residents became less concerned with keeping Fairfax bucolic than with preventing huge tax hikes, their interests coincided more with those of the housing industry. Even if they did not strongly support the developers, their confidence in the board had been shaken by local trends and the industry's public relations campaign. The supervisors evidently had the burden of restoring that confidence in their planning and land use control leadership.

Conclusion

During its first year in office, the board pursued its intention to regulate development more strictly through policymaking. The rezoning moratorium, amendments to the septic tank ordinance, and time-phased issuance of sewer hook-ups were its major policies designed to expand growth control. To reinforce these measures, the board also applied foot-dragging techniques in individual rezoning cases. Although the supervisors channeled some of their efforts into reorienting bureaucratic procedures, they focused on policymaking as a means of consolidating their authority.

These three policies demonstrate the board's preference for autonomous action at the beginning of its term. Undertaken by the board, they were all meant to enlarge its management of growth at the expense of developers and staff. Because the moratorium, septic tank amendments and withholding of sewer capacity were not permanently implemented, the board failed to achieve its immediate objective. But despite judicial rebuffs, the board's efforts were not entirely futile. It maintained an activist stance that court reversals dampened but did not squelch. With respect to the distribution of land use powers, the supervisors' challenge of developers and George C. Kelley produced mixed results. They harassed the housing industry, but lost most lawsuits that questioned the validity of their innovative regulatory devices. This assault ultimately provoked a counterattack that blossomed in the spring of 1973. Furthermore, increasing congestion and assessments, compounded by the industry's publicity campaign, caused a citizen backlash against the board.

While industry victories in court and public outrage over property taxes weakened the board's standing, the county executive's departure tightened its control over county government. Kelley had manipulated public officials in order to establish his personal administration. By precipitating his resignation, the board decisively regained its rightful role as head of the local government.

The supervisors would not have proposed the drastic policies if they were not committed to controlling growth more effectively. Given their resolve, judicial denial of their initial means only convinced them to persevere in their goals, but modify their methods. Their tactical defeats encouraged the evolution of a comprehensive strategy. With a stronger hold on the administrative apparatus and the experience of their first year in office, the supervisors adopted a new approach to affirm their leadership in planning and land use control.

The Planning and Land Use System: Overview

Introduction

PLUS demonstrates the new attitude, approach, and target the supervisors have chosen. Their formerly strident and antagonistic tone has become muted and conciliatory. Their earlier piecemeal, foot dragging maneuvers have been replaced by a cohesive plan for action. Their assault on the housing industry has given way to a shoring up of their own administrative resources. These modifications correspond to three tasks implicit in the PLUS proposal, which are: to build consensus, integrate county growth control activities, and revitalize planning.

These tasks would represent an optimal effort by the board, except that there are qualifications associated with each task. First, the consensus should consist of all groups concerned with growth, yet it excludes the housing industry. Secondly, program development and implementation should be pursued in tandem. However, they are relatively isolated from each other, and agencies once with major responsibility for present land use control have been virtually relegated to positions of observers. Thirdly, planning should be the foundation of growth control, but existing capital facilities overshadow planning as the prime determinant of future development activity. As a prelude to the detailed assessment of PLUS, these three tasks will be described.

Consensus Building

Consensus building is the most crucial of the three tasks that the board has implicitly assumed because the future of PLUS depends on support from key groups in the public and private sectors. Widespread acceptance for PLUS requires extraordinary finesse and diplomacy. Land use control has traditionally been exercised by a broad spectrum: elected and appointed officials, bureaucrats, developers and other interest groups, and citizens. Authority has been divided among these partially autonomous yet interdependent agents.

The boundary between private rights and public responsibility has never been distinct. Now it is even more blurred in localities like Fairfax, where the governing body has proposed a transformation of development regulation. Although the reappraisal and revision of governmental philosophy and practice has just begun, public/private rivalry has already intensified. It seems likely that if PLUS is implemented, different levels of government will compete for the powers wrested from private hands. Thus the board has injected more uncertainty and flux into a controversial and volatile area.

The board has attempted to generate support for PLUS in two major ways. First, it made citizen participation an integral facet of the system. Citizens participate in reviews of most PLUS components through their representation on advisory bodies, attendance at public forums organized by supervisors and staff, and interaction with the Community Liaison Branch of the OCP.

This responsible role assigned to residents serves a dual purpose. On the one hand, it keeps the public informed of county activities and fosters openness in government. On the other hand, it provides the government with alternative perspectives on issues and with proposals that can improve PLUS.

Secondly, the board expressed the PLUS policies in such abstract terms that all interested parties—citizens, developers, officials in state and neighboring local governments—can only accept them. The fourteen policies are subject to conflicting interpretation, but the original language contained in the *Proposal for Implementing an Improved Planning and Land Use Control System in Fairfax County* is unimpeachable. Their sensible yet vague phrasing guarantees unanimous approval. During their first year in office, the supervisors saw their concrete policies, such as the rezoning moratorium, denounced and invalidated. Realizing that these early ordinances were too specific to escape criticism, they ascended to a higher level of abstraction that defied disagreement.

The text of the original task force proposal illustrates the semantic shift that the supervisors achieved. The policies are as follows:

Policy 1:   Quality of Life
Fairfax County is committed to improving the quality of life through local and regional comprehensive planning and development control systems, which facilitate the effective allocation of public resources and shape development patterns.

Policy 2:   Environmental Constraints on Development
The amount and distribution of population density and land uses in Fairfax County should be consistent with the environmental constraints inherent in the need to preserve natural resources and meet Federal, State, and local water quality standards, ambient air quality standards, and other environmental standards.

Policy 3:   Growth and Adequate Public Facilities
Growth in the County should be held to a level consistent with available, accessible, and adequate public facilities as well as with rational plans to provide new public facilities. The County's development plans should take into account financial limitations and administrative constraints associated with increased need for public facilities.

Policy 4:   Adequate Public Services
Fairfax County is committed to provide a high level and quality of public

services for its citizens. Development plans should take into account financial limitations and administrative constraints associated with expanded demand.

Policy 5:   Housing Opportunities

All who live and/or work in Fairfax County should have the opportunity to purchase or rent safe, decent housing within their means. The County's housing policy shall be consistent with the Board's support of the Metropolitan Washington Council of Governments' "Fair Share" formula.

Policy 6:   Employment Opportunities

Fairfax County should encourage employment opportunities with the objective of steadily increasing the proportion of people working and living in the County and of reducing the distance between place of residence and place of employment.

Policy 7:   Programs and Facilities for Quality Education

In order to insure quality education, Fairfax County should provide flexible public educational programs and facilities which effectively meet student and community needs.

Policy 8:   Culture and Leisure Time Activities

Fairfax County should provide full opportunity for all residents to make constructive use of their leisure time through regional and local systems of safe, accessible and enjoyable parks, recreational and cultural programs, both active and passive, and the preservation of areas of historic significance.

Policy 9:   Transportation

Fairfax County should encourage the development of accessible transportation systems designed to move people and goods efficiently through advanced planning and technology with minimal environmental impact and community disruption. Regional efforts to achieve a balanced transportation system through the development of rapid rail, commuter rail, expanded bus service and reduction of excessive reliance upon the automobile should be the keystone policy for future planning and facilities.

Policy 10: Private Sector Facilities

Fairfax County should encourage the development of appropriately scaled and clustered commercial and industrial facilities to meet the need for convenient access to goods, services and employment.

Policy 11: Open Space

Fairfax County should support the conservation of appropriate land areas in a natural state (including small open spaces in already congested and developing areas for passive neighborhood uses, visual relief, scenic value and screening and buffering purposes) to preserve, protect, and enhance stream valley, meadows, woodland, wetlands, plant and animal life through a combination of an acquisition program, a tax policy, the police power and other appropriate means.

Policy 12: Revitalization

Recognizing its commitment to sustain and improve the quality of life, Fairfax County should encourage the revitalization of older areas of the County where present conditions are inconsistent with these policies, and prevent the encroachment of commercial and industrial development on residential areas.

Policy 13: Property Values
Fairfax County should investigate methods to recapture portions of increased property values created as a result of public actions.

Policy 14: Financial Planning and Management
Fairfax County should support equitable systems of taxation and user charges necessary to implement all its policies, recognizing its obligations to provide services and facilities to both established and new developments, and to attract desirable business and industry.[84]

Integration of Innovative Growth Control Activities

In contrast to consensus building through citizen participation and generalized policy statements, the second task focuses on the county government. No matter how much support PLUS has outside of local government, the county must launch a comprehensive campaign to ensure its future viability. There are two main justifications for the unified county effort that PLUS incorporates. First, a government-wide approach promotes bureaucratic consistency, which improves the system's credibility. It also offers a range of measures, some of which are likely to withstand court challenges even if others do not. Secondly, a unified county effort guarantees the staff assistance that the board needs to pursue its objectives. The administrative organization established to develop the PLUS programs and the contents of those programs reflect the board's decision to improve growth control through integrated governmental action.

The management system for PLUS is comprised of nine task forces. There is one task force on PLUS, which supervises the entire project, and eight task forces that correspond to functional areas. These areas are: community facilities and utilities, economics, fiscal and population, environment, housing, land use, transportation, land use control improvement program, and analytical tool development.

The task force on PLUS consists of four supervisors, the deputy county executive, and the directors of Planning and Research and Statistics. The functional area task forces are composed largely of administrative staff, most of whom are drawn from the OCP, Office of Research, and Statistics (ORS), OEA, OMB, and the DCD. Representatives of advisory bodies (notably the EQAC), regional governmental organizations, and state government are also included.

Although PLUS is an interagency endeavor, primary administrative responsibility rests with the OCP. OCP staff comprise over half of the total membership on the functional area task forces. To facilitate the office's role, it was completely reorganized in mid-1973 in conformance with PLUS, and new staff was hired to work on the components. Other agencies involved in PLUS had undergone few, if any, personnel and structural changes as of January 1974.

Linking the policies and task forces are the ten PLUS programs: countywide plan, district plans, capital improvements program, interim development controls, environmental impact statement ordinance, adequate public facilities ordinance, land use control improvement program, new zoning ordinance, citizen participation, and analytical tool development. Most of the functional area task forces contribute toward the development of a countywide, long-range, comprehensive plan. OCP staff, assisted by staff who perform decentralized functions, such as libraries and social services, are responsible for the district plans. The capital improvements program (CIP) is also primarily an OCP assignment, although Research and Statistics and Management and Budget staff also participate.

A land use law consultant assisted by legal researchers is handling the interim development controls (moratoria) and adequate public facilities ordinance. The draft ordinances are reviewed by the task force on PLUS and other staff. The environmental impact statement ordinance is under the jurisdiction of the OEA.

Special task forces were set up for both the land use control improvement program, which includes proposals for land banking and transferable development rights, and analytical tool development, which consists of computer models and a data bank. The new zoning ordinance, commissioned by the previous board, is being prepared in the County Development Department by a zoning consultant assisted by a study committee. Citizen participation occurs in conjunction with all other programs, and the Community Liaison Branch of the OCP has primary staff responsibility for this program.

Revitalization of Planning

Both the administration and contents of the PLUS policies and programs reflect the board's commitment to revitalize planning. In the context of this third task, "revitalization" refers to the original role that state enabling legislation assigned to planning, but which has never been achieved in Fairfax County and most other localities. Planning was conceived as the foundation of land use control. According to the Virginia code:

The comprehensive plan shall be made with the general purpose of guiding and accomplishing a coordinated, adjusted, and harmonious development of the area which will, in accordance with present and probably future needs and resources best promote the health, safety, morals, order, convenience, prosperity or general welfare of the inhabitants.[85]

This ostensible general guide could be implemented by means of a CIP, subdivision regulations, and zoning. But this hypothesized process, whereby planning preceded and directed land use regulation, rarely occurred. In Fairfax County, the role of planning declined to the point where George Kelley transferred responsibility for zoning and other regulatory devices from the Planning Division to the newly created DCD. Thus, while the former county executive abandoned planning because it was irrelevant to him, the board recognized its potentially pivotal function in land use control.

The board's decision to revitalize planning is legally sound and administratively feasible. The board is fulfilling both the letter and intent of the state enabling act by assigning planning a dominant role. Thus the innovative PLUS programs rest on a traditional base. The board successfully modified the personnel, functions, and structure of the Planning Division. In contrast to the housing industry, whose vigorous opposition thwarted the board's early attempts to regulate development, the Planning Division was so demoralized by past emasculation that most staff members welcomed the changes. Thus the board found the planning staff a malleable vehicle for growth control that enhanced the credibility of PLUS.

In addition to the implicit evidence of a revitalized planning process, explicit reference is made to its transformation. On the one hand, the original proposal for PLUS concluded that:

planning must be dynamic, responsive, and systematic . . . The planning function must be an ongoing responsibility of top management and must integrate all municipal activities affecting development in a single, coordinated process.[86]

On the other hand, the first PLUS status report expresses the revitalization of planning as follows:

The dominant characteristic of the PLUS program will be an open planning process with specified times at which all participants can examine . . . the analysis of existing conditions; the policies and objectives statement; analytical studies, countywide plan alternatives; and the drafts of the countywide and district plans.[87]

In other words, PLUS is planning in a variety of programmatic forms.

The three implicit tasks of building consensus, integrating the county effort, and revitalizing planning derive from circumstances peculiar to Fairfax County. For the evaluation of PLUS to serve as a case study, it must be dealt with in a more generalized context. Therefore, PLUS will be analyzed in terms of legitimization, policy formulation, program development, and implementation. Various county publications relating to PLUS delineate its policies and programs. In contrast, general county operations form the basis for assessing legitimization and implementation.

7

The Planning and Land Use System: Legitimization

Introduction

The following analysis represents an interpretation of contemporary events rather than an account of stated objectives and motives. Recent developments in the county government and the political system within which it operates furnish a basis for comparing the probable short run gains and possible long run losses of current legitimizing activities by the PLUS leadership.

To clarify the decisionmaking hierarchy within PLUS, the task force on PLUS with the addition of the county executive will be referred to as the PLUS leadership or directorate. As in all county matters, the full board has ultimate authority. But from an operational standpoint, this group is the decisionmaking core of PLUS. Occasionally the supervisors' goals will be distinguished from those of the senior administrative staff. In many instances, no differentiation is necessary, because the chief elected and appointed officials that comprise the PLUS directorate face similar constraints and forge a common strategy.

The behavior of the Board of Supervisors, county executive, and their principal PLUS advisors is paradoxical. They are building some parts of the political foundation essential to legitimize their innovative growth controls, while undermining others. The explanation lies in their time frame, which is distorted by their concern over the 1975 local election. This focus affects PLUS policies, programs, and implementation as well as legitimation, which both operates independently and pervades the other phases.

According to their schedule, the PLUS policies and programs should be completed in the spring of 1975, when election campaigning swings into high gear. The supervisors apparently want a finished product that they can take credit for in the race that most incumbents have lost over the past fifteen years. There is nothing sinister about this objective; re-election is a natural political preoccupation. The potential harm is that by tending to ignore the more distant future, they may reap a blighted harvest for the county.

Given a mid-1975 election deadline, the PLUS leadership has established four primary aims. The first is consolidation of public backing for PLUS. Secondly, it seeks to resolve PLUS-created competition among the supervisors and senior administrative staff. Thirdly, it wants to avoid conflict between agencies charged with designing PLUS and those that are peripherally involved yet significantly affected by it. Finally, it seeks to exclude or minimize participation by actual or potential rivals of the county government in local growth control, such as the housing industry and state and neighboring local governments.

Citizen Participation

As mentioned earlier, PLUS decisionmaking incorporates the county residents. Specifically,

Citizens will be involved through a variety of mechanisms, including contact with existing groups, work sessions with groups established by the Supervisors, open public forums at the countywide and district levels, citizen surveys and a variety of written media.[88]

Decentralized communication in the form of staff presentations and staff/citizen discussions conducted throughout the county is programmed for over 20 percent of the seventy-four 'major milestones' of the PLUS work schedule.[89]

Citizen participation requires modification of existing procedures as well as introduction of new ones. The board rearranged its schedule so as to devote one monthly meeting to PLUS. In December 1973, for instance, staff presentation of the PLUS quarterly progress report took place in the evening to maximize public attendance.

Not only board operations but agency staffing also reflects the supervisors' interest in citizen participation. In particular, personnel changes in the OCP demonstrate this concern. James Reid was selected as director of this agency in part because of his commitment to community involvement. Before joining the county government in mid-1973, Reid was an official of the Hartford Process, an urban renewal program that emphasizes citizen participation. In keeping with the original proposal for PLUS, he established a Community Liaison Branch "specifically responsible for enabling continuous citizen involvement in all phases of the work."[90]

The extent to which Reid's orientation is shared by his colleagues will determine if the proposals for citizen participation constitute empty rhetoric or genuine intent. Whether community involvement amounts to the window dressing or foundation of PLUS, it is evidently a major concern of the directorate.

**Rivalry Among Agencies with
Major Responsibility for PLUS**

While citizen participation is a positive element that the PLUS leadership is cultivating, rivalry among senior officials is a negative by-product that it must minimize. From a functional viewpoint, inter-agency competition could disrupt PLUS operations and delay scheduled completion of its policies and programs. In substantive terms, the outcome of this rivalry will determine the orientation and distribution of responsibility for growth control. For both of these reasons, the PLUS leadership has a vital stake in settling disputes that arise. Initial disagreement centered on two PLUS components: citizen participation and analytical tool development (modeling).

The first topic of contention was citizen participation, which emerged early and was settled quickly. This confrontation pitted the Board of Supervisors against the county executive and director of Comprehensive Planning. The supervisors evidently wanted to dominate this aspect of PLUS, and Wilson and Reid wanted to prevent this outcome.

The initial task force report specified board leadership in organizing citizen participation, but left the staff role vague. Community involvement at three levels was proposed: countywide, district, and planning area. While the county-wide and district boundaries were obvious, the configuration of the planning areas was ambiguous. They did not coincide with the planning districts, which were already accounted for. But a very definite connection could be drawn between the planning areas and magisterial districts, since there were eight of each. The chairman of the board was responsible for the countywide effort, and the other supervisors for their districts. In contrast, Community Liaison/Technical Assistance Teams were delegated general duties, but no definite jurisdiction.[91]

This ambiguity apparently derived from an unreconciled disagreement as to the status of this OCP staff. As events unfolded, it became clear that the board wanted planning areas to coincide with magisterial districts as a means of supervising the planning team assigned to each district. In contrast, the county executive and planning director wanted this staff accountable to the bureaucracy. Within three months after the PLUS projects was adopted, they reached the following compromise: planning districts conform to magisterial boundaries, and citizen participation is conducted at the countywide and district levels. This arrangement facilitates the district supervisors' interaction with planning staff, but keeps the director of the OCP in charge of their activities.

The second subject of dispute is modeling or analytical tool development, the most controversial and as yet unresolved element of PLUS. In this instance, the director of the OCP and the director of the ORS support different approaches. While Planning favors a limited role for modeling, Research and Statistics envisions it as a major undertaking. Both the scope and significance of this component were scaled down, primarily due to board and public reactions to modeling.

The original task force report on PLUS devoted 44 out of 160 pages to this element, which was introduced as modeling. This lengthy sales pitch can be associated with three main factors. First, the report was prepared by ORS, which handles most computerized data collection and systems analysis for the county government. Secondly, modeling is the single most costly item in the PLUS budget: $500,000 out of a total of $1,500,000.

Thirdly, ORS has a skeleton in the modeling closet, which PLUS will modify: the Urban Development Information System (UDIS). Envisioned as a comprehensive land use planning device, UDIS has actually severely restricted capabilities. It catalogs current data on population, land uses, sewer and water lines, and real estate assessments. No attempt is made to either formulate projections or evaluate actual development. To compensate for these shortcomings, ORS staff interpret the system's results using other germane information, such as market conditions. Expansion of its data base and operations to make the Urban Development Information System more inclusive and versatile is part of PLUS modeling.

Given these circumstances, the ORS launched a major public relations campaign to improve the image of computer technology in Fairfax County. This effort achieved overexposure, which produced heated discussions in several board sessions and community meetings during mid-1973. ORS staff defended the component by explaining that the board would continue to make final decisions about land use. Skeptics, who feared that computers would replace elected officials at the controls, wanted to know why the county was spending $500,000 to maintain the current decisionmaking process.

Disagreement over modeling, which began during the summer of 1973, had led to a tentative compromise by January 1974. First, the directors of Planning and Research and Statistics share responsibility for modeling, whose role and visibility have been curtailed. Ultimate decisionmaking authority rests with the OCP, but its director has chosen not to impose his views.

Secondly, semantics and editing were applied to reassure the public. The term 'modeling' was purged from the PLUS vocabulary and replaced by 'analytical tool development'. To remove still more of its technological stigma, the component is referred to primarily by its product: "analytical studies." In addition, mention of the total cost of the component is avoided.

Thirdly, the $30,000 pilot program conducted by consultants, originally conceived as a preliminary phase of analytical tool development, was changed to a feasibility study. A massive modeling effort had become a possibility instead of a foregone conclusion.

Thus the technocrats, as one Northern Virginia newspaper dubbed ORS, achieved mixed results. The analytical tool development component was approved with its initial budget but a lower profile. Although it was placed under the immediate control of ORS, Planning supervises the component. The findings of the consultants' feasibility study and staff research will determine if the full amount allocated for analytical tool development is spent. In sum, there seems to be a consensus in the county that, as the original task force report contended:

Through information storage capabilities, the proposed planning system can far outstrip the analytical capabilities of traditional, intuitive planning methodologies.[92]

Conflict between Agencies with
Primary and Peripheral Roles in PLUS

While the PLUS leadership has dealt with internal rivalry, it has largely ignored competition between agencies with primary and peripheral responsibility for the new project. Despite changing staff assignments, it is possible to identify two groups of agencies connected with PLUS: the insiders or PLUS-involved agencies, and the outsiders, or PLUS-affected agencies. Although both groups participate to varying extents in PLUS operations, the insiders play a dominant role in decisionmaking, while the outsiders are relegated to a subordinate status.

This relatively stable distribution of authority places the Board of Supervisors and Offices of the County Executive, Comprehensive Planning, Research and Statistics, Environmental Affairs and the county attorney, the Planning Commission (PC), and the EQAC in firm control of PLUS policy and program development. The minor powers include the DCD and DPW, water and park authorities, and school board.

Agencies such as County Development and Public Works, which enforce conventional county land use regulations, have been denied a significant role in formulating the innovative controls to avoid dissension. There are substantive and procedural grounds for conflict between the insiders and outsiders. The PLUS-involved agencies are proposing an approach to development regulation that contradicts attitudes held by the PLUS-affected agencies. To institutionalize their new approach, the insiders are establishing programs that require different skills, functions, and structures within the county bureaucracy. Under a reorganization, the outsiders, whose operations have become irrelevant at best and detrimental at worst, are bound to be disrupted, demoted, or replaced.

This threat to the established bureaucracy is exacerbated by the composition of the insiders' and outsiders' leadership. Most of the top staff positions in the PLUS-involved agencies are filled by newcomers to Fairfax County. For example, the county executive and his deputy, county attorney, and directors of Comprehensive Planning and Environmental Affairs joined the bureaucracy after 1971. In contrast, many senior officials in the DCD and DPW are veterans with ten to twenty years service, often in the same line of work. Also, many top staff members in the PLUS-affected agencies are either natives of Fairfax or long time residents, unlike many of their counterparts in PLUS-involved agencies. These differences in background and experience deter communication and understanding.

The philosophical and occupational gulf between the PLUS-involved and PLUS-affected agencies makes competition inevitable. Whether this tension explodes or dissipates depends on the transition from past to future governmental operations. At present, the PLUS directorate is postponing a confrontation by largely sidestepping the issue. Limited measures have been instituted to expand the role of some outsiders. For instance, the Water and Park Authorities were included on the expanded Task Force on Planning and Land Use Control. But the apparent policy governing PLUS policy and program development is that no transition will be made.

The decision to by-pass intergovernmental rivalry relating to PLUS decision-making carries definite short-range benefits and potential long-range liabilities. By skirting the problem of agency competition, the directorate can proceed more efficiently with policy and program development. Attempts to share information, reconcile differences, or win converts involve staff time that would delay operations or make them more costly if additional personnel were needed.

The desire to postpone rivalry between PLUS-involved and PLUS-affected agencies accounts partly for the present lack of emphasis on implementation. If the directorate specified the administrative apparatus required to carry out the PLUS programs, it would have to repudiate the current organization. Major modifications of established procedures are implicit in PLUS, but until they are verbalized, the outsiders cannot raise concrete questions. Lacking tangible evidence that their positions and functions are threatened, they have no recourse but to wait for the ax to fall. Only when the new administrative machinery is unveiled will they be in a position to challenge it and defend themselves.

Unfortunately for the PLUS leadership, the phases in progress—policy refinement and program development—will not last long enough to ease out bureaucratic opponents and abolish their vacated positions. So while it can defer interagency competition, it cannot eliminate its using the present avoidance tactics. At best, when the full impact of PLUS is revealed, conflict will be as severe as if the problem were dealt with before the implementation stage.

It is more likely, however, that delay will heighten anxiety and frustration among staff members who sense their agencies becoming anachronistic. Under such circumstances, alienated employees will probably resist change more strenuously. The ensuing bureaucratic battle could hamper implementation of PLUS and even paralyze county growth control.

To prevent this confrontation, it is recommended that discussions on program implementation between insiders and outsiders be initiated by mid-1974. The PLUS directorate, which is covertly considering various administrative arrangements, should schedule meetings to explore the general administrative concomitants of PLUS and present alternative reorganizations. Based on these sessions, the PLUS leadership should devise an interim administrative structure to prepare staff for the forthcoming transformation. No positions would be eliminated, but functions and organization would be changed to conform with PLUS policies and programs. The major alterations would occur as program development nears completion, tentatively in mid-1975.

**County Treatment of Other Political
Participants with Potential Influence
on PLUS**

Introduction

Unlike the three other goals, the PLUS leadership's neglect of elements in the political system beyond county control concerns long-range returns. It opted for short run benefits in dealing with public backing, rivalry relating to contents of PLUS, and conflict between PLUS and traditional development regulatory agencies. In contrast, the directorate evidently decided that its long-range interests require barring participation by the housing industry and minimizing involvement by state and neighboring local governments. It will be shown that this view is shortsighted and either may promote unfavorable actions or discourage helpful measures by these entities. A broader perspective and appropriate activities will be proposed to alleviate these potential drawbacks.

The Local Housing Industry

The PLUS directorate has instituted a policy of benign neglect toward the local housing industry. Developers are neither represented on advisory bodies dealing with growth control nor in groups established by supervisors to review PLUS components. Only one oblique, negative reference was made to them in the PLUS publications that appeared during 1973:

Many of these decisions affecting the nature of the County's development, the quality of housing, and the character of its neighborhoods are made in the private sector or by individual citizens. Our program can only provide guidelines for affecting some of these activities, in many circumstances; in other instances, the combination of controls and incentives will have a profound effect on private decision-making. A program that fails to distinguish between these implementation factors could raise expectations far beyond our capacity to deliver.[93]

Developers rightly feel that they have been excluded from public decision-making regarding PLUS. Their forum for communication with the board and administrative staff is the public hearing, where substantive deliberation does not occur. The board's policy has thus replaced confrontation with avoidance. Although this approach appears to insulate PLUS from industry involvement, it may actually increase developers' influence over implementation in the long run.

The major advantage of preventing constructive participation of the housing industry is that the PLUS directorate would avoid compromising the policies, programs, and implementation time-table for the present. As of early 1974, the board was under pressure from two main groups in the county population: those who felt it has reneged on its promise to curtail growth and those who reject this goal. Proponents of the board's position are in the majority, but opponents are becoming a more vocal minority. This criticism is encouraged by developers, who have expanded their focus on lawsuits to include public demonstrations by construction workers and others whose livelihood depends on growth.[94] The supervisors value the allegiance of their supporters more than placation of their detractors, and thus they refuse to moderate their stand. This approach will reassure their backers, whose confidence was shaken by judicial rebuffs and rising taxes, but it may frustrate their critics to the extent that they assume a more extreme position in the future.

By rejecting political bargaining during the policy and program development stages, the directorate is inviting legal challenge. As of early 1974, over 100 lawsuits challenging board actions relating to PLUS had been filed. Even though the county staff and consultants are attempting to ensure the validity of PLUS, there are few legal precedents in Virginia cases for many of the innovative measures. Thus the county's position in court will be somewhat tenuous. Because the PLUS leadership is giving the housing industry no alternative but to a courtroom confrontation, it is risking the entire Planning and Land Use System.

In most legal proceedings, the aim is to maximize differences as a means of proving that one party is right and the other wrong. This adversary process is antithetical to political interaction, where the parties must compromise in order to coexist. Since development is likely to remain a joint public/private endeavor in the immediate future, caution would dictate sacrificing some philosophical purity for the opportunity to practice innovative growth control.

To preclude the zero-sum game characteristic of lawsuits, the PLUS directorate should modify its treatment of developers. Basically, it should solicit their views and inform them of PLUS activities. Specifically, representatives of the housing industry should be included on the Task Force on Planning and Land Use Control—the major PLUS deliberative body that incorporates members of the public and private sectors. In addition, county advisory bodies that deal with growth control on a more general level, especially the EQAC, should expand their members to encompass the housing industry. Finally, board members should regularly address organizations representing developers, such as the Northern Virginia Home Builders, just as they speak to other community associations.

These recommendations will ensure a substantive industry contribution to PLUS. In and of themselves, however, they will not resolve major differences between the local government and the housing industry. Undoubtedly, there will be strong disagreement, but without the hostile atmosphere that has characterized their courtroom and public hearing encounters. They may, nonetheless, eliminate the apprehension and antagonism that ignorance generates by furnishing a normalized communication network. They may also facilitate the task of forging a workable compromise between the county and developers, whose positions are presently frozen.

State and Neighboring Local Governments

Just as the PLUS leadership shuns an active role for the housing industry, so it seeks to minimize participation by the state government and neighboring localities. It exhibits a "fortress Fairfax" mentality toward these elements of the political system because it feels that their interference can only hamper PLUS. This suburban isolationism is not total since representatives of state and metropolitan agencies are involved in specific PLUS components. But it is stronger than changing conditions in local governance warrant.

The directorate is resisting the tide of mushrooming state and metropolitan involvement in local planning and land use control. Two noteworthy examples are the Planning District Commissions that Virginia authorized to promote regionalism and the "fair share" formula that the Washington, D.C. area Council of Governments devised for allocating low and moderate-income housing construction on a metropolitan-wide basis. This trend is likely to intensify rather than diminish, and it is contended that Fairfax County's long-term interests are best served by anticipation rather than by avoidance. Specifically, PLUS implementation may be assisted by the state legislature or hindered by neighboring jurisdictions, and a broader role for both groups may benefit the county's growth control efforts.

Presently the state and area local governments have a limited technical or functional role in PLUS. Representatives of the Virginia Department of Highways, Northern Virginia Planning District Commission, Northern Virginia Transportation Commission, and Washington Metropolitan Area Transit Authority serve on PLUS functional area task forces.[95] In addition, a PLUS-sponsored meeting on innovative growth controls included members of the Virginia Assembly Legislative Committee on Land Use.[96]

The PLUS leadership has refused, however, to encourage broad political participation by the Virginia legislature or the Metropolitan Washington Council of Governments. It is recommended that these groups be granted advisor or observer status, while PLUS decisionmaking would remain in local hands. This role might help promote potential positive action by the Virginia legislature and deter possible detrimental measures by the metropolitan jurisdictions. The possibilities that the state would take steps to damage Fairfax or that area localities would try to assist the county are more remote and therefore will not be explored.

If lawsuits challenging PLUS programs are successful, the county may seek support in state enabling legislation. With Virginia code amendments, the constitutionality of its measures would be enhanced, and it would largely only have to justify their particular application. On the one hand, Fairfax County could attempt to have prescriptive portions of the code, such as the administration of zoning, modified to permit more diversified land use regulation. On the other hand, it could try to have innovative techniques, such as time-phased development, added to the list of permitted growth control devices. State legislators would probably be more favorably inclined toward these proposals if they knew more about PLUS.

Alternatively, neighboring localities might interpret PLUS as exclusionary and an effort by Fairfax County to promote its welfare at their expense. Since Fairfax's low and moderate-income housing stock and minority population are very small, area jurisdictions could claim that limited growth discriminates against poor blacks, who are under-represented in the county. In protest against Fairfax's unilateral decision to allow its neighbors to accommodate this segment of the region's population, they could contest PLUS in court.

Although the outcome of such a suit is uncertain, the Michigan State supreme court established a precedent that supports the potential plaintiffs. In *Bristow v. the Town of Woodward*, the prohibition of trailer parks in the local zoning ordinance was invalidated on the grounds that it prevented lower income persons from becoming residents of the community.[97] Thus the court placed the interests of the metropolitan area above those of the individual jurisdiction. It seems that such a situation could be more readily avoided if Fairfax County's neighbors were informed of the specific impact of PLUS.

To prepare for these possible scenarios, the PLUS directorate should expand communication with the state legislators and public servants in neighboring localities. First, a publication explaining the basic goals, contents, and operations of PLUS should be produced and distributed to these officials. In addition, the PLUS leadership should prepare an edition of the quarterly progress report, which is circulated in the county government, for external use.

Secondly, discussions between Fairfax County and other state and local representatives should be held to permit a thorough exploration of PLUS. For example, county officials might address the state legislature, regional planning districts, and the local Council of Governments, which would ensure broad audiences. These sessions should be open to the public, and citizen participation in discussions should be encouraged.

Finally, the PLUS leadership should invite localities to send delegates to Fairfax County for a firsthand survey of PLUS activities. The directorate has sought or welcomed nationwide publicity on PLUS and made presentations to Virginia officials who requested information on its growth control efforts. But it has yet to take the initiative in promoting these activities on a metropolitan or state-wide scale. The county would retain complete jurisdiction over PLUS, but these consultations with state and local governments may convince it to shift priorities and reorient programs in ways that are ultimately of mutual benefit.

Conclusion

Thus the PLUS leadership is pursuing lopsided legitimization by concentrating on public support and the PLUS-involved agencies, and by neglecting the PLUS-affected agencies, housing industry, and state and neighboring local governments. This focus expedites PLUS policy refinement and program development, but may jeopardize implementation. To promote the successful completion of all four PLUS phases, it is recommended that the directorate expand its legitimating activities and pursue optimal long run, as well as short run results.

8

The Planning and Land Use System: Policymaking

Introduction

The interim development and redevelopment policies serve the PLUS leadership's legitimization effort well. They represent the comprehensive, countywide approach that replaced the unilateral and fragmented actions of the board's first year in office. The fourteen policies respond to the major concerns voiced by county residents and public officials. Their phrasing is abstract and general in order to generate widespread acceptability and thereby build consensus for PLUS. They contain ambiguities and inconsistencies that in the context of legitimation are virtues and must be preserved.

But policymaking is also an end, a distinct phase of the governmental process. While the policies provide a means of achieving legitimacy, their primary function relates to decisionmaking. In order for the policies to assume their stated role as a guide for public action, their ambiguity and inconsistency must be diminished. They must give direction yet be vague, because complex bureaucracies require administrative discretion. They must set priorities yet be somewhat contradictory, since democratic governments represent constituencies with conflicting goals and priorities.

As this explanation of the necessary ambiguous and inconsistent aspects of policies implies, policy refinement occurs simultaneously with program development and implementation. Although these phases of the governmental process overlap, policymaking can also take place outside the context of specific programs and administrative machinery.

These two settings produce distinct forms of policy refinement whose differences are relative but nonetheless significant. Policies that surface within the political as opposed to bureaucratic context are more goal-oriented and normative and reflect philosophical considerations. In contrast, those that emerge through administrative operations are more program-oriented and descriptive and indicate technical analysis. Elected officials and citizens are more likely to perform goal-oriented or normative policy refinement and bureaucrats, program-oriented or descriptive policymaking.

It is contended that policymaking must be separated from, as well as linked with, program development and implementation. Only independent refinement can provide policies with a different perspective that enables them to offer direction or at least criticism of governmental activities. To allow policies to perform this crucial function, it is suggested that goal-oriented policy refinement consist of three sequential steps.

First, assumptions and value judgments underlying the policies must be identified and evaluated. Second, the contents of the policies must be assessed in terms of accuracy and completeness. Any deficiencies revealed by these two steps must be corrected. Third, the policies must be ranked in order to establish a priority system to guide program development and implementation.

The PLUS directorate recognized that the interim policies, in their original form, were inadequate as a guide for public action. It incorporated both types of policy refinement in the PLUS work program devised in mid-1973. However, subsequent PLUS operations and publications reveal that the leadership has departed from the work program in such a way that goal-oriented policy refinement has not and ostensibly will not actually occur.

After tracing the demise of normative policymaking, the fourteen interim development and redevelopment policies will be analyzed. This analysis will aim to detail the three-step policy refinement process. The policies will not actually be refined because it is felt that the board and citizens of Fairfax County must undertake this task. Rather, the decisions that normative policymaking entail will be set forth in an attempt to stimulate this process.

The Derailment of Normative Policymaking

Based on the record, it is difficult to ascertain why goal-oriented policymaking was abandoned. Members of the PLUS directorate were evidently either ambivalent or in disagreement about the issue because they produced some highly confused opinions. Four documents relating to PLUS contain statements that indicate muddled thinking on whether or not to perform normative policy refinement. However, over the six-month period they span, the confusion gradually diminished to the point where the decision is discernible. In chronological order, the documents are: *A Proposal for Implementing an Improved Planning and Land Use Control System in Fairfax County* (Proposal), the first PLUS quarterly status report, a memorandum on staff task forces, and the second PLUS progress report.

The *Proposal* which was adopted in June 1973, deals with the application and refinement of the interim policies as distinct and simultaneous steps. The policies are intended to provide criteria for board decisionmaking, guidance for staff work, and direction for private sector investment planning.[98] Alternatively, the proposed planning and land use system is supposed to develop "quantitative objectives and criteria to assist in policy analysis . . ."[99] Furthermore, according to the suggested PLUS time table, the formulation of standards, criteria, goals and objectives is continuous, and its ultimate purpose is to assist staff in preparing plans.[100]

The board and Planning Commission, as well as administrative staff, are involved in this process, set in an operational context. It is therefore unclear whether goal or program-oriented policy refinement is intended. Thus the philosophical and technical aspect of policymaking are confused, and normative policy refinement appears to be pre-empted in the development of standards and criteria that pertain to PLUS objectives.

The first PLUS status report, issued in September 1973, reiterates the policy applications described in the *Proposal* and compounds the confusion between goal-oriented and program-oriented policymaking. On the one hand, the report states that the Board of Supervisors will establish priorities for analytical studies.[101] On the other hand, it states that analytical priorities will emerge from staff review of the issues.[102] This represents circular thinking: policies are supposed to direct analysis of existing conditions and trends, and existing conditions and trends are supposed to shape policies. One of these alternatives must take precedence over the other.

In the PLUS work program that the report sets forth, policy refinement is first submerged in the staff assignment to analyze existing trends and conditions and later surfaces discretely as an outcome of this process. Although the semantic subtleties preclude definitive interpretation, it appears that descriptive policy refinement in an operational framework will prevail.

This conclusion of technical primacy is reinforced by the November staff memorandum. It assigns PLUS staff responsibility for analyzing existing conditions and trends and reviewing board policies in order to identify issues and establish priorities for analysis. Not only will initial policy refinement be performed by staff and thus minimize philosophical considerations, but staff will use data that resulted from approaches and procedures PLUS is replacing.

This situation highlights the need for goal-oriented policymaking in Fairfax County. Since PLUS represents a new outlook on growth control, there are no appropriate administrative guidelines for program-oriented policy refinement. Decisions based on technical considerations cannot conform to the new outlook, because it has yet to be institutionalized. For staff to revise policies dependent on information derived from an approach that PLUS rejects is a denial of PLUS and a reversion to past programs.

The December PLUS status report confirms the primary staff role and therefore the dominance of program-oriented policy refinement. Although the interim development and redevelopment policies will be discussed at public forums chaired by supervisors and commented on in writing by citizens, their practical application is in staff hands. Specifically, "the policies are being reviewed at the staff level to determine how they can be utilized to provide guidance for the PLUS program and how they can be translated into more detailed objectives, standards, and criteria."[103]

Since the public forums and staff review occur more or less simultaneously and independently, policymaking has evidently been delegated to staff. On the one hand, staff will not receive citizen input in time to incorporate it in their analysis. On the other hand, different branches of the OCP have basic responsibility for citizen participation and policy analysis. The Community Liaison staff handle the former and the Public Facilities staff the latter, with little interaction. Thus goal-oriented, normative policymaking is reduced essentially to a ceremonial endeavor.

It is important to speculate as to whether the confusion over goal-oriented policymaking was motivated by ambivalence or disagreement among the PLUS directorate. The leadership could have been ambivalent because it recognized the role of normative policy refinement, but feared that the process would cause the consensus, cemented partly by the abstract language of the policies, to disintegrate. Alternatively, the directorate could have been divided, with board members favoring normative policymaking and staff members opposing it. Since staff prepared the last three documents cited above, it is easy to see how its views could have eluded board scrutiny given their barely perceptible presentation.

Naturally, if the motivation were ambivalence, it would be harder to obtain a reappraisal of the decision than if it stemmed from disagreement. In the first case, the PLUS leadership would be united and committed to a common course of action. In the second case, the board members would be amenable to a review of the staff assignment. Although these two motivations affect the difficulty of performing goal-oriented policy refinement, neither diminishes the need for it. To illustrate this need, a procedure for refining the PLUS policies based on philosophical rather than technical issues will be explained.

The Interim Development and Redevelopment Policies

Introduction

In accordance with the three-step policy refinement process, the analysis of the interim policies will deal with implicit assumptions and value judgments, flaws and omissions, and juxtaposition of demands and prerequisites for growth and no-growth. The fourteen policies will be grouped into seven functional categories to facilitate the identification of assumptions and value judgments.

They will be criticized for defects and gaps mainly on an individual basis. The specification of trade-offs implicit in the dual focus on development and environmental protection will concentrate on pairs of policies. This analysis is not intended to be comprehensive and exhaustive. Its purpose is to raise enough questions about the policies in order to demonstrate the necessity of goal-oriented policymaking. Therefore, a sample of assumptions and value judgments, deficiencies, and trade-offs will be explored.

*Implicit Assumptions and Value
Judgments*

Introduction. Implicit assumptions and value judgments will be approached from both broad and narrow perspectives. On the general level, two pervasive indicators of inherent preconceptions and biases are the pledge of direct county action to achieve a policy and the mention of costs associated with a policy. They are either included or excluded from the delineation of each policy and reflect a basic set of priorities. Policies that express direct county measures are considered more vital than those the local government only supports. Alternatively, policies whose concommitant costs are cited have stronger limitations imposed on them than those whose costs are not cited, and therefore the former are less significant.

On the specific level, each policy contains key but vague phrases that require interpretation based on preconceptions and biases. Some of these phrases will be quoted in order to show the role that assumptions and value judgments play in policy refinement. This analysis accepts the presence of subjective assessment and does not challenge the contents of particular preconceptions or biases. Its aim is to heighten awareness of their contribution and encourage evaluation of them in terms of the many possibilities that the PLUS policies presently omit.

Analysis of Functional Areas. The seven functional areas that form the framework for appraising preconceptions and biases are: financial and land use planning and controls, public facilities and services, environmental protection, educational and leisure time activities, housing and urban renewal, employment opportunities, and transportation. The policies will be referred to by number and abbreviated title (for the full citation, see pages 62-64). Table 8-1 summarizes the county attitudes and priorities implicit in the policies.

The three policies listed in the financial and land use planning and controls category are: policy 1—use of planning and development controls to improve the quality of life, policy 13—exploration of ways to limit excess profits due to public action, and policy 14—financing of PLUS through taxes and user charges. They all entail direct county steps, and policy 1 excludes any reference to costs, which is the subject of policy 14. Since both policies 13 and 14 deal with financing, the issue of mentioning costs is moot.

Phrases whose interpretation depends on assumptions and value judgments include: "improving the quality of life" and "effective allocation of public resources" in policy 1, "Portions of increased property values" in policy 13, and "desirable business and industry" in policy 14.

Public facilities and services comprises two policies: number 3—basing growth on the availability of adequate public facilities, and number 4—basing growth on

Table 8-1
The Interim Development and Redevelopment Policies: Implicit Governmental Commitments

Functional Areas and Policies	Administrative Commitment		Financial Commitment		Rank of Composite Commitment		
	Direct Action	Support	No Mention of Cost	Cost Cited	High	Medium	Low
Financial and Land Use Planning and Controls							
No. 1 – Quality of life	X		X		X		
No. 13 – Property values	X		–		X		
No. 14 – Financial Planning and management	X		–		X		
Environmental Protection							
No. 2 – Environmental constraints on development	X		X		X		
No. 11 – Open space	X		X		X		
Educational and Leisure Time Activities							
No. 7 – Programs and facilities for quality education	X		X		X		

No. 8 – Culture and Leisure time activities	X	X	X
Public Facilities and Services			
No. 3 – Growth and adequate public facilities	X	X	X
No. 4 – Adequate public services	X	X	X
Transportation			
No. 9 – Transportation	X	X	X
Housing and Urban Development			
No. 5 – Housing opportunities	X	X	X
No. 12 – Revitalization	X	X	X
Employment Opportunities			
No. 6 – Employment opportunities	X	X	X
No. 10 – Private sector facilities	X	X	X

the availability of adequate public services. These policies involve direct county efforts and refer to financial and administrative costs. Preconceptions and biases are critical in defining the following statements: "take into account financial limitations and administrative constraints" in both numbers 3 and 4, "available, accessible, and adequate public facilities" in 3, and "high level and quality of public services" in 4.

Environmental protection incorporates two policies: number 2—establishment of environmental constraints on development and number 11—promotion of open space. This category calls for direct county intervention and omits reference to associated costs. Highly connotative phrases in these policy statements are: "the need to preserve natural resources" in policy 2 and "appropriate land areas" in policy 11.

There are two policies in the education and leisure time activities category: number 7—provision of programs and facilities for quality education, and number 8—provision of cultural and recreational programs and facilities. Both policies express an active county commitment and make no mention of required expenditures. Assumptions and value judgments are applied in the definition of "quality education" and "flexible public education programs and facilities" in number 7 and "constructive use of their leisure time" in number 8.

Two policies fall under the heading of housing and urban renewal: policy 5—adequate housing at reasonable costs for county residents and workers and policy 12—revitalization of older areas while protecting residential neighborhoods. This category indicates public support and does not refer to the associated costs of the policies. Phrases that invite a range of connotations based on preconceptions and biases are: "the opportunity to purchase or rent" and "consistent with the Board's support of the . . . 'Fair Share' formula" in number 5 and "present conditions are inconsistent with these policies" and "encroachment of commercial and industrial development" in number 12.

The transportation category contains only one policy, number 9, which involves development of a regional system emphasizing mass transit. Direct county action, as part of a metropolitan-wide effort, is pledged, and physical and social costs are cited. Assumptions and value judgments are implicit in "minimal environmental impact and community disruption," "balanced transportation system," and "excessive reliance upon the automobile."

Employment opportunities encompasses two policies, numbers 6 and 10, that respectively deal with an increase in the number of persons who live and work in Fairfax County and accessible commercial and industrial facilities. Public backing for these policies is offered and no mention of attendant expenses is made. Phrases that provide a range of interpretation, based on preconceptions and biases, include: "steadily increasing the proportion of people" and "reducing the distance" in policy 6 and "appropriately scaled and clustered" and "convenient access" in policy 10.

Ranking of Policies. Based on this selective review of assumptions and value judgments, the policies can be divided into three groups that indicate relative importance. The following seven policies are ranked highest, because the policy statements pledge direct county action, and make no mention of costs. They can therefore be considered the county's major commitments: policy 1—quality of life, policy 2—environmental constraints on development, policy 7—programs and facilities for quality education, policy 8—culture and leisure time activities, policy 11—open space, policy 13—property values, and policy 14—financial planning and management.

Policies 3—growth and adequate public facilities, 4—adequate public services, and 9—transportation comprise the middle level of governmental concern. They entail county action limited by consideration of associated costs. Unlike the highest ranking policies, which also require expenditures, this middle group is deemed more dispensable because the cost factor is included in the policy statement and thus curtails pursuit of the anticipated gains.

Finally the lowest ranking of the county's priorities, as implied by the phrasing of the policies, are: policy 5—housing opportunities, policy 6—employment opportunities, policy 10—public sector facilities, and policy 12—revitalization, which only received public endorsement and encouragement.

This three-tiered grouping reflects the county's explicit goal of managed growth: a stronger commitment to facilities and services for residents (7 and 8) rather than newcomers (3 and 4), and no-growth (2 and 11) rather than development (5, 6, and 10).

Defects and Omissions

Apart from the debatable merits of the assumptions and value judgments that created the ranking, some of the interim policies contain deficiencies that call their validity into question. Policies 3, 4, 5, 6, 10, and 12 will be assessed in light of local conditions that challenge their feasibility, omissions, and faulty logic. Policies 3 and 4, 5 and 6, and 10 and 12 will be discussed together, as they exhibit related flaws.

Limiting growth to the availability of public facilities and services, the aim of policies 3 and 4, is a reversal of the decisionmaking process. These policies represent the deterministic orientation that the board has ostensibly abandoned with its adoption of PLUS. The language of these policies indicates that the level of public facilities and services is fixed and that development must be accommodated to the existing or planned capacity. In reality, the amount of facilities and services is a variable within environmental bounds. The county establishes this amount based on the level of future development it sets.

The implication that public facilities and services determine growth distorts actual capital improvements planning, in which population projections yield required levels of facilities and services. Policies 3 and 4 erroneously indicate that this issue is beyond public control. This tendency to shun responsibility for decisions on residential land use denigrates PLUS, because it shows a lack of commitment to the basic premise that a local government can manage growth.

Policies 5 and 6 express support for objectives whose implementation would require extensive private investment in direct contradiction of PLUS's basic aim of slowing the growth rate. Local employment and housing trends present major obstacles to pursuing these policies. In terms of 1970 commuting patterns, roughly 64 percent of Fairfax County residents presently work outside the jurisdiction,[104] and 37 percent of those who work in the county are non-residents. From the standpoint of housing, 70 percent of the county residents cannot afford the average price of a new home, and county residents are wealthier on the average than most of their neighbors.[105]

Since Fairfax County has promised to curtail growth, the substantial new residential, commercial, and industrial development and the expansion of housing and employment opportunities involved makes policies 5 and 6 unattainable. Furthermore, massive public financial assistance would be required to permit residents to obtain housing, and the local government has not accepted this burden. With reference just to the low and moderate-income segment of the housing stock, the county is already 950 units behind on its "Fair Share" pledge.[106] Thus, the evidence points to a serious lack of commitment to carrying out these policies.

Policies 10 and 12 represent extremes in terms of their treatment of residential development. Policy 10 omits residential development altogether, even though it is the dominant private land use in the county and a critical aspect of convenient access to goods, services, and employment. Furthermore, housing units need guidance with respect to scale and placement at least as much as the commercial and industrial facilities cited in the policy statement.

In contrast to this neglect of residential development, an over-emphasis on this type of land use in policy 12 seems to preclude its main purpose: revitalization. This policy prohibits the encroachment of commercial and industrial land uses on residential neighborhoods, a process that the economics of urban renewal and the composition of Fairfax County's older communities necessitates. On the one hand, urban redevelopment is so expensive that without massive public subsidies, commercial and industrial facilities must often replace housing units to help defray the costs. On the other hand, Fairfax County's older areas, where revitalization is needed, all contain a substantial amount of residential development. Therefore, a revitalization effort that did not cause some encroachment would be extraordinary. Thus the soundness of both these policies is rather dubious considering the characteristics of the local housing supply.

Contradictions and Trade-offs

The fourteen interim policies are not only dependent on diverse assumptions and value judgments for their meaning and are deficient, but they are also incompatible and in some instances mutually exclusive. Theoretically, there is an inverse relationship between any two policies, since public funds are limited, and to allocate more money for one policy is to take money away from another. To narrow this range of possibilities to a more significant sample, only the trade-offs involving policies that utilize similar approaches and/or address comparable subjects will be discussed. These criteria create three types of trade-offs: between costs and benefits of growth, competing costs, and competing benefits. All of the trade-offs assume that development entails expenditures and yields benefits. In addition, the latter two types assume a governmental commitment to curtail development.

The first type of trade-off that the policies demand concerns the costs and benefits associated with development. There are four major cases where this form of contradiction emerges. The first is between policies 1—quality of life and 2—environmental constraints on development. The first policy advocates the distribution of public resources, while the second proposes conservation of natural resources.

Although the term "public resources" is vague, it is reasonable to assume that either natural resources are a form of public resource, or to obtain man-made public resources some natural resources must be expended. In the first case, allocating public resources is a benefit that requires using natural resources, a cost. In the second case, preserving natural resources is a benefit that prevents the allocation of public resources, also a cost. Thus since each policy must be sacrificed to achieve the other, they are to some extent incompatible.

Secondly, policies 3—growth and adequate public facilities and 4—adequate public services, on the one hand, and 7—quality education facilities and programs and 8—cultural and leisure time activities, on the other hand, refer to the costs and benefits of development. Policies 3 and 4 indicate the administrative constraints and financial cost of expanding public facilities and services that must be taken into account in any development project. In contrast, policies 7 and 8 offer the benefits of educational, cultural and recreational programs without mentioning associated costs. The expenditures are inseparable from the facilities and services: a cost reduction produces a decrease in benefits and likewise an increase in benefits involves rising costs. Hence the policies are to a degree conflicting.

Thirdly, the costs cited in policies 3 and 4 can also be weighed against the benefits from new development expressed in policies 5—housing opportunities and 6—employment opportunities. In this instance, the expenditures are required to generate the gains of personal convenience and comfort and energy conservation. If more residents of Fairfax County work in the county and more persons employed in the county live there, commuting can be curtailed. Consequently, some of the money, time, gasoline, and environment expropriated from transportation can be saved and diverted to other activities. The administrative constraints and financial costs of providing facilities and services for new development are offset by the personal and environmental benefits of new residential, commercial, and industrial construction. Higher costs yield greater benefits, and lower costs fewer benefits. Therefore these two pairs of policies are mutually exclusive in a certain extent.

Finally, policies 10—private sector facilities and 12—revitalization are contradictory to some degree. Commercial and industrial facilities are an asset, according to policy 10, when they afford convenient access. But they become a liability that must be avoided in policy 12, when they threaten to encroach on residential neighborhoods. In some older areas of the county, therefore, revitalization will have to exclude commercial and industrial development, or the construction of commercial and industrial facilities will have to threaten residential development. Thus, as in the first example, private sector facilities and the preservation of residential communities serve as both gains and losses in relation to each other. And in either case, they are somewhat incompatible, since the cost of one is counterbalanced by the benefit of the other.

The second and third types of trade-offs that the policies generate involve either costs or benefits of growth. One case in which the lesser cost and two in which the greater benefit must be selected will be presented. Focusing on the debit side of the growth equation, policy 9—transportation and policy 3—public facilities—incorporate costs that must be weighed against each other. With reference to transportation, environmental impact and community disruption must be minimized, whereas in the case of public facilities, administrative constraints and financial costs must be considered. A rating of these two policies would require a relative appraisal of their limitations. From the standpoint of reducing the burden on the community, these policies are thus to some extent mutually exclusive.

Turning to the credit side of the growth equation, housing and employment and financial management exemplify the choices that must be made between various benefits. Policy 5 advocates expanded housing opportunities and policy 6 expanded employment opportunities. Yet because the county is committed to reducing its growth rate and interjurisdictional commuting is the rule, these benefits compete with each other for limited development capacity. In other words, the demand for both increased residential, commercial, and industrial land uses exceeds the supply of sewer hook-ups, rezonings, and other services that the county is now rationing. A choice must be made between housing and employment opportunities, because too much growth would be necessary to accommodate both policies fully. Therefore, they are to a degree incompatible.

Policies 13—increased property values and 14—financial management and planning reflect the proverbial desire to have one's cake and eat it too. On the one hand, Fairfax County wants to discourage speculation and has proposed to explore ways of recapturing the increased value of property due to public action. On the other hand, it is anxious to attract desirable business and industry. These benefits contradict each other. Excess profit that the local government wants to reclaim is the incentive required to attract investors, who would provide support for business and industry to locate in the county. Some speculative gains would have to be sacrificed in order to obtain desirable commercial and industrial development. Thus the two benefits are somewhat mutually exclusive.

Conclusion

The assumptions, biases, and trade-offs described above indicate the ambiguities, omissions, and inconsistencies in the interim development and redevelopment policies. This sample assessment was designed to present a need for goal-oriented policymaking by pinpointing some of the unresolved issues that the current phrasing raises. The three-step normative policy refinement process is essential in order for the policies to fulfill their dual function as guides for PLUS and preliminary aims that can be translated into objectives, standards, and criteria. Without analysis of the assumptions and value judgments implicit in the policies, correction of their deficiencies, and the establishment of a priority system to accommodate their inherent contradictions, the interim policies will neither be able to give direction nor perspective to PLUS.

To ensure that the fourteen policies perform their stipulated roles, it is recommended that goal-oriented policy refinement take place. Before the PLUS programs are adopted in final form, the Board of Supervisors and citizens should clarify the interim policies based on philosophical considerations. Goal-oriented policymaking should occur through citizen participation vehicles established for PLUS. Advisory bodies and community organizations, as well as individual residents, should contribute to policy refinement. The board must determine the priority system for the policies in light of public comments, since it is closer to the people and more removed from specific programs than the PLUS staff. Thus it can more readily assume the normative viewpoint vital to the task.

9

The Planning and Land Use System: Program Development

Introduction

The PLUS programs reflect the tortuous conversion in development regulation that Fairfax County is making. They encompass the refinement of traditional land use controls and adoption of innovative ones enacted by other localities. Although on an individual basis many of the programs have definite merits, collectively they pose the problem of incongruence. Some derive from divergent orientations toward land use control and involve incompatible means and ends. Others represent similar attitudes and there is a resulting duplication of activities.

The lack of synchronization created by this juxtaposition of conflicting and overlapping programs results from uncritical eclecticism. On the one hand, conventional regulatory devices, such as zoning, are retained without questioning their relationship to innovative controls, such as the EIS and APF ordinances. On the other hand, novel techniques, for example, transferable development rights and land banking, are borrowed wholesale, rather than evaluated in light of local conditions and adapted accordingly. Certain links between individual programs are recognized and dealt with, but no effort is made to identify the full range of interaction among all the programs. It seems that the political aim of pleasing special interests that occurred during the initial stages of PLUS overrides the professional aim of creating a cohesive operation.

This analysis sets PLUS implementation as the primary consideration and will explore deficiencies that emerge both in individual programs and between these various programs. As of early 1974, most of the programs were in preliminary form. Thus it is only feasible to assess their broad purposes and functioning and to make general recommendations.

Since citizen participation supports all the programs and analytical tool development supports some of the programs, their evaluation extends beyond their individual boundaries. The following programs will be appraised on a comparative basis: countywide comprehensive plan, district development plans, EIS ordinance, APF ordinance, CIP, and zoning ordinance. Finally, the legality and practicality of moratoria, transferable development rights, and land banking will be assessed.

Citizen Participation and Analytical Tool Development

Citizen participation and analytical tool development are treated in tandem because of the philosophical polarization they represent. The general public is by

93

definition non-professional, whereas modeling is the apex of technical sophistication. Ostensibly community involvement underlies PLUS, but it is impossible to
expect average county residents concerned about development regulation to
possess expertise essential to review the analytical tool development program.

Apart from their diametrical opposition, each program contains a major flaw
that may impair its individual effectiveness: administrative fragmentation in the
case of citizen participation and indeterminate contribution in the case of
analytical tool development. These defects stem from a common problem
explored in the discussion of implicit board goals and PLUS legitimization:
bureaucratic in-fighting over the contents of both programs and over the
distribution of operational responsibility for them. Following an assessment of
their individual deficiencies, the fundamental incompatibility between citizen
participation and analytical tool development will be addressed. Recommendations for remedying their separate and interrelated defects will be made.

Citizen participation is intended to provide public scrutiny of all other PLUS
components through countywide and district forums, existing advisory bodies,
new groups set up by supervisors, and the activities of the Office of Comprehensive Planning's Community Liaison Branch. This plethora of administrative
mechanisms encourages disjointed, uncoordinated, and overlapping functions.
The program's multi-dimensional structure may weaken and even dissipate its
impact.

PLUS demands more intensive community involvement than the county
government pursued in the past, and countywide and district forums, groups
formed by supervisors, and the Community Liaison planning staff were initiated
to supplement existing public entities. However, the resulting administrative
apparatus is so intricate, it tends to become amorphous. It is recommended that
available machinery, namely the PC and EQAC, be adapted to respond to new
needs by subsuming some of the proposed organizational instruments. These two
advisory bodies are assigned responsibility for citizen participation, but given the
multitude of vehicles, their actual role is ambiguous.

The PLUS directorate should tap rather than by-pass the potential of the PC
and EQAC for expanded community involvement. It is proposed that the board
dispense with special groups. Furthermore, the countywide and district forums
should be merged into a single operation that falls under the combined
jurisdiction of the board, PC, EQAC, and Community Liaison Branch. Since the
first three governmental entities have representatives from each magisterial
district and one at-large member, they fulfill the geographic concommitant of
the forums. Committees based on geographic representation and functional
expertise, through rotation of Community Liaison staff and other EQAC
members, would coordinate the citizen participation activities of all four
governmental bodies. Both of these proposals are aimed at increasing the
functions of the PC and EQAC by eliminating alternatives that are not necessary.

There are two main advantages to simplifying and coordinating the administrative apparatus of citizen participation. First, these steps will reduce duplication, competition, and inconsistency that is inevitable when too many agencies share common authority. Secondly, they will reinfoi e the advisory bodies that will continue to pursue citizen participation under PLUS implementation. Public review will diminish when program development ends, and a smoother transition between these two phases will be achieved if temporary structures do not have to be dismantled, but only permanent ones have to readjust. For these reasons, the PC and EQAC deserve to play a more prominent part in citizen participation.

In contrast to citizen participation, substantive and procedural activity surrounding analytical tool development is negligible. Due to public skepticism regarding models, the program has assumed a profile so low that only a faint outline can be seen. This slight trace reveals a major defect of prematurity with respect to other PLUS programs, apart from the general criticisms of modeling cited earlier.

Analytical tool development is intended to monitor local conditions in order to contribute to comprehensive plan and CIP preparation and updating. However under the existing schedule, these latter components will be drafted before analytical tools are forged. The timing of the development of plans and analytical tools also calls into question the modeling effort's appropriateness. Until planning is completed, it is difficult to decide what information to collect and the type of analysis that will be needed.

It is therefore suggested that the scope and timing of analytical tool development be altered to conform with these planning activities. Specifically, the program should be initiated after the plans and CIP are adopted and generate data suitable to them. In this way, analytical tool development can provide relevant support to PLUS.

The most troubling aspect of citizen participation and analytical tool development is not their individual flaws, but their contradictory points of view. Increased reliance on public review and computer technology are mutually exclusive, since neither vehicle can readily accommodate the other. Most county residents are ignorant of systems analysis, and systems analysis utilizes a frame of reference indifferent to county residents.

There is no total solution to this inherent incompatibility, since the nature of local urbanization requires additional community involvement and data processing. On the specific level of PLUS programs, separate domains can be carved out for citizen participation and analytical tool development. For instance, residents should review policies, and computers should monitor variables for the CIP. The problem is that citizen participation involves less tangible, quantifiable and malleable elements than analytical tool development, and it is therefore easier to focus on the latter than the former.

To ensure a balanced perspective on these two conflicting yet vital programs, it is recommended that their respective roles be clearly delineated and that the board conduct periodic assessments of their operations. The board, responsible to the electorate for local governance, is uniquely capable of mediating between citizen participation and analytical tool development.

The Countywide Comprehensive Plan and District Development Plans

The original proposal for PLUS proclaimed that a systematic and dynamic planning process formed the system's underpinning. However, the juxtaposition of a countywide comprehensive plan and district development plans may undermine this foundation. Planning in the context of PLUS is supposed to provide flexibility to modify the decisionmaking framework.[107] Yet this flexibility is apparently reserved for the district level plans, since they form the basis for public and private actions affecting "citizen concerns, development, the environment and the allocation of public resources."[108] In contrast, the countywide, long-range, comprehensive plan will be structured along traditional lines with functional components sketched in vague outline. The plan is bound to be rigid and irrelevant because the fluidity and responsiveness that could have been engineered into it has been channeled to the district plans.

These two types of plans encompass approaches that the county has pursued in the past. A countywide, comprehensive plan was enacted in 1938 and a major revision occurred twenty years later. In 1962, the board divided the county into fourteen planning districts to address localized issues. Planning proceeded at the district level during the 1960s, largely in response to, rather than in anticipation of, development pressures. This operational link between planning and development was formalized in the adoption of short-range, development-oriented planning, administered by the DCD. The formation of this agency and introduction of this type of planning reflected the sterility of comprehensive planning as practiced in Fairfax County.

The architects of PLUS's dual level planning process envision a "healthy tension" between long-range, countywide issues and short-range, localized requirements. However, it seems the outcome may be truncated planning that will produce unnecessary and counterproductive conflict. First, the existence of two types of plans serves to widen the gap between professionals and citizens, since citizens are likely to be more interested in the district development plans. The countywide and district plans are intended to ensure input from centralized and decentralized sources, but separate information channels rather than two-way communication may emerge. As they did in the past, proponents of long and short-range objectives will probably ignore or attempt to by-pass each other if they have different programmatic vehicles.

Secondly, if responsibility for countywide and district plans is divided between two departments or two divisions within the OCP, rivalry among the professional staff is more likely than cooperation. Both the divergent issues the two planning forms address and the bureaucratic necessity of delimiting unique domains will magnify differences between the countywide and district plans. The distinctions essential for administering this bifurcated planning process will tend to generate a lack of coordination. Thus separate long-range, comprehensive and short-range, localized plans seem to jeopardize the revitalization of planning that is a central facet of PLUS.

For Fairfax County to achieve a "meaningful planning capacity,"[109] it is recommended that the two types of plans merge into a single planning process. Instead of utilizing the countywide plan as a basis for separate district plans, PLUS should make the countywide plan a multi-faceted instrument that incorporates detailed proposals for subunits. This unified planning process would promote synchronization in two respects.

On the one hand, district segments would conform more closely to the countywide plan than separate plans because they would share the same data base and result from coordinated staff work. Whether the present comprehensive planning staff expanded its operations to handle the short-range components or new staff was assigned this task, the work would proceed in an integrated manner.

On the other hand, district plans would probably mesh better with each other if they were all part of a single process, rather than elements of a distinct planning program. The unique characteristics imputed to the district plans deserve special attention, but the creativity that the current program design diverts to them can be more profitably channeled into a single, diversified planning system.

A final contribution that this unified planning system can make relates to the delineation of sub-units for detailed study. The existing planning districts derive from earlier patterns of development, as well as topographical features. A re-evaluation of these boundaries and the choice of criteria for sub-units are vital ingredients of a dynamic and relevant planning process. A single, integrated set of plans is more likely to promote the development of an innovative and comprehensive information system than the two types of plans included in PLUS. Under the suggested merger, the planning data bank would require modifications because it would serve a new program with different needs, instead of two revamped programs with set precedents. If the district plans are prepared, a critical assessment of their boundaries is less likely, since each will be dealt with distinct from the others.

Because the planning data base determines what is known, it influences what is done. It must therefore anticipate future trends rather than mirror past conditions. A new, unified plan will promote this function more readily than two-level planning that stems from previous county efforts. For these reasons, the comprehensive and localized plans should be replaced by a multi-dimensional planning program.

The Environmental Impact Statement
and Adequate Public Facilities Ordinances

Like the countywide and district plans, the proposed EIS and APF ordinances demonstrate the fragmentation of overlapping and complementary land use controls. According to common usage, "environment" denotes physical elements, both natural and manmade, and social, economic, and cultural elements. Therefore, an EIS incorporates the adequacy of public facilities from two standpoints.

First, it deals with the effects of development on the natural environment, specifically air, water, and noise pollution. Secondly, it addresses the effect of development on the human population, both residents of surrounding areas and those who will live and/or work in the proposed projects. In particular, requirements for water and sewer lines, schools, recreation facilities, and fire, police, and social services would be determined.

Based on their similar focus, the EIS and APF ordinances could be merged. Short run legal and political considerations, however, apparently dictate the administrative separation of environmental impact from capital improvements, the foundation of the APF ordinance. This proposed arrangement may, however, damage the long-term management of growth.

The EIS is already an accepted land use control. EIS's are required by many federal agencies and are incorporated in Fairfax County's RPC and planned development zoning categories, although perhaps not in the precise form envisioned by PLUS staff. Thus this regulatory device requires neither state enabling legislation nor public education to convince the housing industry, residents, and other interested parties of its validity.

On the other hand, ordinances that tie the amount and rate of growth to adequate public facilities have only been enacted on a limited scale, and the acceptability of this control in Virginia is uncertain. Despite its dubious status, an APF ordinance is potentially stronger than an EIS ordinance, which accounts for the former's special appeal to local governments. An APF law that ensures time-phased development, such as the Ramapo controlled growth ordinance, provides significant additional discretion to a local governing body. Whereas the EIS law enforces quality standards in development, an APF ordinance would permit public staging of growth. The former is a negative control that can prevent harmful development; the latter, a positive control that can dictate where and when development will occur.

Perhaps to avoid jeopardizing the EIS requirement by including the increased powers that the APF ordinance confers, the PLUS leadership has made these two controls independent. Separate legislation is being drawn up for each of these regulatory devices and different county agencies were assigned responsibility for them. The OEA is charged with developing machinery for implementing the EIS law, and the OCP and ORS and DCD are to handle the APF law. This arrangement invites lack of communication and synchronization.

Since the EIS and APF ordinance contain common elements, bureaucratic functions will overlap. Governmental departments are ordinarily reluctant to divulge data they collect, as knowledge affords power, or at least leverage. Sharing information used to perform comparable operations threatens agencies' domains even more than when they handle different subject areas and activities. Although uniform standards are proposed for evaluating environmental impact and the adequacy of public facilities where they converge, agency rivalry is likely to hamper coordination. Furthermore, this division of administrative responsibility will probably encourage duplication of effort.

To prevent these difficulties from disrupting implementation of these crucial land use controls, a legislative and administrative merger of the EIS and APF ordinance is recommended. The EIS is the conceptually broader of the two controls, and it should be expanded to incorporate time-phasing of growth and other specific provisions that link the APF law to the CIP. A separability clause should be included in the EIS legislation to help promote implementation of the environmental impact portions of the law, since a controversy over staging of development could arise.

Administrative consolidation should accompany this legislative integration. To guarantee a single set of guidelines for environmental impact regarding the adequacy of public facilities, the four agencies delegated responsibility for the EIS and APF ordinance should collaborate on program development. The OCP, which supervises PLUS and is preparing the CIP, should coordinate the effort that also involves the OEA, ORS and DCD.

The Capital Improvements Program
and Planning

A key vehicle for implementing the countywide and district plans and justifying the APF ordinance is the CIP. In theory, development of the CIP should follow adoption of plans and precede enactment of the APF law. But Fairfax County has departed from this format under PLUS, and the OCP is preparing a preliminary CIP spanning five years before formulating the comprehensive and development-oriented plans. A second CIP, covering twenty years, will be prepared after the countywide and district plans are adopted, the APF ordinance is enacted, and the PLUS policies, objectives, and criteria are finalized. The first CIP was scheduled for completion in January 1974, and the final version in January 1975.[110]

The fact that the final CIP will be formulated after planning is completed indicates the importance of basing the CIP on adopted plans. Unfortunately, the division of the CIP development process into two stages may lead to a reversal of roles. Namely, the CIP could determine the contents of the plans, which would weaken PLUS.

Several political considerations may have influenced the decision to rely on the two-part process for drawing up the CIP. First, county agencies were accustomed to preparing their capital budgets for the next fiscal year based on their own goals and data. These budgets were submitted to the OMB, which reviewed agency requests in light of criteria chosen by its staff or the Office of the County Executive. Little effort was made to designate a common set of guidelines. Under PLUS, however, capital improvements budgeting requires long-range projections, and evaluation is transferred from the OMB to the OCP. The Public Facilities Branch established a standard procedure and uniform criteria for agencies to follow. The preliminary CIP gives agencies the opportunity to adjust to the new operation before embarking on their twenty-year budgets.

Secondly, the two-phase CIP development process may expedite enactment of the APF ordinance. The foundation of the APF legislation is the CIP, which indicates the present and planned availability of public facilities and thus demonstrates the county's efforts to provide necessary services to residents and businesses. Since the original PLUS timetable specified adoption of the APF ordinance in March 1974,[111] the preliminary CIP would be ready to substantiate its regulatory provisions. Without split preparation of the CIP, the APF ordinance would lack evidence that the county anticipates future development, a factor that weighed heavily in the court case involving the model for the county's law: Ramapo's controlled growth ordinance. By the time the APF law is implemented, the twenty-year CIP should be completed.

Notwithstanding the benefits of acclimatizing county agencies and justifying the APF legislation, the two-stage preparation of the CIP presents three potential drawbacks, which should be recognized and avoided in order to fulfill the goals of PLUS. In particular, the PLUS commitment to planning that is oriented toward decisionmaking and to citizen participation may be at stake. Possible negative effects of completing the preliminary CIP before the long and short-range plans are prepared will be identified. Then modifications of the work program and other safeguards designed to minimize these effects will be proposed.

First, partially reversing the order of CIP and plan preparation may weaken the status of planning in Fairfax County. Although the first CIP is preliminary and only deals with a five-year period, the tendency to base the countywide and district plans on it may arise. The temptation to develop plans that mesh with the CIP, rather than ignore CIP and face possible contradictions between these PLUS components, will be strong.

While plan preparation may be easier if the initial CIP serves as a guide, the purpose of planning will be subverted. Instead of charting a course for future public facilities and by extension development, the countywide and district plans may become mere rubber stamps for the CIP. The timing of CIP and plan formulation may therefore undermine planning—a blatant contradiction of the board's implicit goal of revitalization.

Specifically, completion of a preliminary CIP before plans are adopted may reinforce a tendency that characterized previous county land use control: physical determinism. As the essence of PLUS policy indicates, the condition of natural resources and public facilities limits development. This statement expresses the inaccurate attitude that natural resources and public facilities are factors that the local government cannot control. It is implied that they are givens that the county must accept and base its decisions on.

In reality, the county makes a significant impact on both natural resources and capital improvements. By interspersing CIP and plan preparation, PLUS may encourage the passive self-image that the county is vacillating about maintaining or discarding. The CIP, conceived in the state code is a tool for implementing the comprehensive plan, may become the foundation of local planning. Ironically, this staging of PLUS components may hamper the dynamic planning process that PLUS was intended to embody.

Essentially, flanking the development of countywide and district plans with a preliminary and final CIP may encourage officials and citizens to base the future on the past. Since policies, guidelines, and criteria will not be delineated when the preliminary CIP is prepared, planners must apply standards derived from previous experience and their personal judgment. If planning becomes a justification rather than a basis for the CIP, then past policies and guidelines and individual staff opinions will determine future projections. In view of the urban sprawl that characterized most local development in the 1960s and the PLUS pledge of community involvement in land use control, this alternative is hardly desirable. Excessive dependence on the preliminary CIP may thus perpetuate trends that PLUS was designed to alter and foil one of its integral elements.

To prevent meaningless planning, physical determinism, and reliance on past policies and trends, the PLUS directorate must maintain a long-range perspective on growth regulation. While the continuation of these tendencies may facilitate completion of certain PLUS programs, they could impair or even negate the contribution that PLUS is supposed to make. The countywide and district plans must be reviewed independently of the CIP by staff, the board, and citizens. There is sufficient local awareness of the damage that past procedures and attitudes caused to avoid their recurrence if the PLUS leadership takes steps to promote vigilance.

The New Zoning Ordinance

Despite tensions among the countywide and district plans and the CIP, APF ordinance, and EIS, these land use controls complement each other. They all have the capacity to promote active public management of growth and thus are integral to PLUS. In contrast, the new zoning ordinance is largely extraneous to PLUS. Prepared by the Zoning Ordinance Study Committee (ZOSC) and by staff from the DCD, it was commissioned by the previous Board of Supervisors. This study committee superceded another advisory body, established in 1965, whose findings were rejected by the board that took office in 1968.

Thus the new zoning ordinance represents the culmination of an effort initiated nearly a decade ago. The magnitude of this undertaking partially justifies retaining its product. This new law is a consolidation and simplification of its predecessor, which over a period of fifteen years has accumulated a plethora of use districts and thousands of map amendments. Differences of emphasis rather than intent characterize the new zoning ordinance.

Zoning embodies an antiquated philosophy of development regulation, yet its presence may either hinder or help PLUS. In several respects the new zoning ordinance is redundant and even detrimental because it restricts governmental responsibility more than the proposed EIS and APF ordinances. However, it is also an accepted regulatory device that the county may have to resort to if developers file suits against the innovative PLUS components and delay their implementation. The new zoning ordinance may also help promote acceptance of other PLUS programs among skeptical county employees and members of the public.

In terms of its contents, the new zoning ordinance is basically superfluous. Its aims are not only accomplished but surpassed by the EIS and APF ordinances, which employ more effective methods. Zoning's fundamental purpose is to regulate the placement and quality of land uses. The EIS and APF laws not only perform these functions, but they also control the level and timing of growth. Furthermore, as exemplified by the county's new ordinance, zoning is plagued by internal contradictions that warrant its demise.

The original means by which zoning pursued its ends was segregation of land uses in order to protect some from harmful effects of others. This approach proved unduly restrictive, and localities turned to mixed use districts, such as the planned development zones in the new zoning ordinance. Planned development-type categories enable public officials to review proposals on an individual basis and impose special conditions. Heavy reliance on planned development categories in the new zoning ordinance is a tacit acknowledgment that rigid use districts are unsuited to modern urban life.

Inflexibility is engineered into zoning through specifications for minimum lot sizes, setbacks, etc., as well as demarcated use districts. To counterbalance some of these arbitrary restrictions, the new zoning law, like its predecessor, includes performance standards. Thus the defects endemic in zoning rob it of direction, continuity, and, in effect, utility.

In contrast, the APF and EIS laws accomplish more than zoning and without contradictory provisions. First, both controls require consideration of individual development proposals based on general guidelines. This case by case assessment eliminates the tension between use districts and planned development options, specifications and performance standards, that characterizes the latest zoning law. Secondly, the EIS ensures that new development will mesh with surrounding land uses.

Thirdly, the APF ordinance regulates the density of residential, commercial, and industrial development by adhering to the size and spacing of capital improvements specified in the CIP. Finally, the APF law replaces the presumption of growth intrinsic in the rezoning process with time-phasing of development. It is a marked improvement over zoning, because it allows the local government to decide the pace of growth. Thus the EIS and APF ordinances are stronger land use controls than the zoning ordinance, since they have expanded its powers and discarded its unnecessary restrictions and inconsistencies.

Nonetheless, the new zoning ordinance may serve as a power reserve for the county government because it attempts to institutionalize PLUS. First, the law will only be redundant when the more innovative PLUS components are implemented. Should housing industry representatives challenge the validity of the APF ordinance in court, for instance, the PLUS staff will have to at least delay exercising the control it grants. An unfavorable judicial ruling would nullify the law's impact, unless or until the county enacted legislation that met the court's approval. During such a period of limbo, the zoning ordinance could prove vital as a source of public authority.

Secondly, including the zoning ordinance in PLUS may facilitate a useful transition from conventional to innovative land use control. Its presence might reassure citizens or private groups who question a radical departure from past practice and make PLUS more palatable to them. Because of its familiarity, the new zoning ordinance might encourage skeptics to assess each program on an individual basis, rather than make a blanket condemnation of PLUS.

Finally, the zoning ordinance may have been added to PLUS as a means of mollifying the County Development staff and other public officials who view zoning as the mainstay of development regulation. Several County Development staff members served on the ZOSC and prepared the draft ordinance. The major PLUS assignment given to County Development is completion of the new zoning ordinance.

According to the work program, "the Department of County Development will be responsible for mapping the new categories in the revised zoning ordinance."[112] This task, which entails rezoning every parcel of land in the county, is scheduled to begin in June 1974 and last for one year.[113] Incorporation of the zoning ordinance in PLUS thus provides work for the agency staff, whose operations had shrunk to the point where many employees were virtually idle by March 1974. This assignment might make them feel more a part of the county's growth control effort.

Its legal and administrative assets notwithstanding, the revised zoning ordinance falls outside the mainstream of PLUS and symbolizes a lack of faith in Fairfax's innovative approach to growth management. The powers it grants to public officials, continuity it may create between past and present procedures, and workload it generates for the DCD may justify its adoption in the short run. But these potential political benefits may become liabilities that can hamper PLUS on a long-term basis. The zoning law may expedite completion of the PLUS programs by mitigating criticism of the system, but it can burden implementation in two crucial respects.

First, by guaranteeing public regulation of development if lawsuits block implementation of other PLUS elements, the zoning ordinance may become a substitute for PLUS. In other words, the back-up control could replace the system. The history of new town development in America furnishes an instructive analogy.

While new towns were originally conceived as economically, socially, and culturally self-contained, most are located near or in major metropolitan areas. Developers and public officials were not convinced that this new urban form was viable. They therefore planned new towns as satellites that could rely on neighboring communities for employment, shopping, and recreation. Consequently, most new town residents work outside their predominantly residential communities like other suburbanites.

Hence the economic safeguard of situating new towns near urban centers expressed a doubt that became a self-fulfilling prophecy. It seems that Fairfax County could also choose the easier alternative, which would be so available. This temptation should be removed, so that it does not have to be resisted.

Secondly, the zoning ordinance may place the local government in the uncomfortable position of possessing a control that it does not want to use. Montgomery County, Maryland offers a prime example of the dilemma improved zoning administration can cause for a locality that seeks broader responsibility to regulate growth.

The Montgomery County Council established the position of zoning hearing examiner under recently enacted state enabling legislation. It appointed two lawyers to perform the quasi-judicial function of reviewing rezoning applications. Staffing this office became difficult in mid-1973, however, because the council frustrated former hearing examiners by deferring action on many cases.[114] This impasse between hearing examiners and a majority of council members revolves around their divergent values and standards.

The attorneys reflect the permissive attitude toward growth that zoning engenders. Essentially, the very existence of use districts presumes that development will occur. In contrast, a majority of the council advocates restrictive management of growth as indicated by the APF ordinance it adopted after creating the office of zoning hearing examiner. Even though the Environmental Protection Agency had imposed a sewer moratorium upon Montgomery County that blocked new growth, the council did not want to grant rezoning applications because they created pressure for future development.

Thus the improvement of zoning in a jurisdiction similar to Fairfax County in size, socio-economic characteristics, and public reaction to urban sprawl has handicapped effective land use control. To guarantee consistent management of growth, the philosophical and administrative anomaly of zoning should be precluded.

Since the new zoning ordinance may either replace some PLUS programs or produce conflict within the system, it should be abandoned and plans to rezone the county should be dropped. It threatens the long-range vitality of PLUS and wastes staff time and county revenues during the current program development stage. Furthermore, the proposed law cannot provide the public controls contained in the EIS and APF ordinance, but it can become an instrument of opposition to PLUS. Fairfax County should openly acknowledge the futility and possible danger of revising zoning and rescind this anachronism of planning.

Interim Development Controls
(Moratoria)

The interim development controls program, which would permit the board to institute temporary rezoning moratoria in portions of the county, is subject to various criticisms, some of which were leveled at the revised zoning ordinance. This program has one major asset that the zoning ordinance lacks: it is temporary. Public reliance on this concommitant of zoning is due to terminate when the other PLUS programs are implemented. The disadvantages of this program, nonetheless, seem to outweigh its advantages. Basically, interim development controls can be challenged in terms of both validity and practicality.

With respect to legal issues surrounding rezoning moratoria, there are two precedents in Fairfax County land use control. Countywide rezoning moratoria were imposed in 1960 and 1972. The first moratorium stemmed from the inadequacy of the zoning ordinance's residential classifications and lasted nine months. During this time, planning staff developed additional multi-family housing categories and detailed specifications for their application. The second moratorium was based on the inadequacy of the comprehensive plan, and it was invalidated by the circuit court. In the earlier case, developers and property owners stood to gain from the expanded regulations and did not object to the moratorium. However, they viewed the later moratorium as an infringement on their rights and successfully contested it.

The proposed interim development controls closely resemble the overturned moratorium, since they derive from deficient plans and will restrict housing industry operations. They differ from the 1972 ban, however, in one major respect. Whereas the previous moratorium affected the entire county, the proposed bans apply to selected areas. This distinction may reduce the arbitrariness associated with the 1972 ban on rezonings. Nevertheless, the two moratoria are similar enough that the judicial decision in the recent case cast doubt on the legality of interim development controls.

In addition to their uncertain legal status, the practicality of the interim development controls is dubious. It seems that two present board policies minimize initiation of new development projects, which is the objective of rezoning moratoria. The first is board denial of rezoning requests, and the second is County Development refusal of sewer hook-ups to development that would be served by overloaded treatment plants. Since little excess sewer capacity exists in the county, there is a de facto building ban that makes a rezoning moratorium largely redundant.

With respect to rezoning applications, the board can refuse most on the ground that sewage facilities are unavailable. It appears that technical flaws could provide the basis for denying some of the remaining applications, leaving few that deserve to be granted. And even those rezoning requests that are approved will not necessarily result in new growth.

Although in the past granting a rezoning application amounted to a public commitment to development, PLUS includes measures that afford an alternative interpretation of this board action. The APF and EIS laws, which should be in effect by the time most future construction would begin, authorize evaluation of development proposals based on more restrictive criteria than the zoning ordinance contains. Thus in light of present and anticipated land use regulations, the interim development controls are essentially superfluous.

Given their tenuous legality and practicality, interim development controls should be abandoned. They represent an expenditure of county resources that is unnecessary at best and counterproductive at worst. If this program takes effect, it will make no substantial contribution to interim growth control. Alternatively, if it is challenged in court and overturned, it will have been in vain.

The program also deserves to be shelved because it derives from zoning. Moratoria on rezoning applications epitomize the rigidity and awkwardness of this anachronistic regulatory technique. There is no way to moderate zoning. It either proceeds or stops, robbing the local government of the maneuverability needed to manage growth. Moratoria detract from the innovative orientation of PLUS and should therefore not be instituted.

**Transferable Development Rights
and Land Banking**

In contrast to rezoning moratoria, which is a fairly routine type of control, transferable development rights and land banking have been applied mainly on an experimental basis in only a few localities. However, criticism regarding practicality and legality can also be leveled against these innovative measures.

Transferable development rights (TDR) involve the completely novel concept of permitting property owners to vary the intensity of use allowed on their land by purchasing and selling development rights amongst themselves. The local government initially establishes the maximum amount of growth that will occur in the jurisdiction, namely the total TDR. This total is then distributed among all property owners, who engage in private market transactions regarding land use.

Land banking, within the context of PLUS, entails public purchase of private property at prices that reflect normal rather than inflated values. Land acquired in this manner would be resold to developers for specified private uses, such as low and moderate-income housing, at a future time determined by the county. The land bank is intended to hold down land prices as a means of reducing speculative profits and promoting land uses that are less attractive to developers.

It would seem that both TDR and land banking require state enabling legislation, as neither private reallocation of land uses nor public participation in the private land market is currently permitted. Technical obstacles that the county would confront in implementing these regulatory devices make the prospect of obtaining Virginia code amendments bleak.

First, TDR and land banking require local officials to predict the future, an undertaking that consultants, bureaucrats, and other experts have bungled dismally in the past. Demographic and economic projections are notoriously unreliable and inaccurate, particularly when derived for a single jurisdiction in a metropolitan region. Too many intervening factors that cannot be anticipated influence trends.

Yet TDR requires that the county establish a limit to growth, and land banking necessitates a public assessment of which areas will yield the highest returns to speculators. The difficulty of making these predictions is further compounded by partial governmental control over growth. Although PLUS enables the county to expand land use control, development will remain a joint public/private venture. Since public regulation will not replace the market place, the county will only be able to influence trends. Consequently its controls cannot be completely effective. Secondly, the projection of the future on the minute scale of individual property holdings, intrinsic to both TDR and land banking, diminishes governmental flexibility. By assigning TDR and forming a land bank, the county makes commitments that it may later want to modify or rescind. These subsequent changes might be liable to charges of arbitrariness or discrimination, and the locality might have to abide by decisions that it could have avoided with less rigid controls.

Thirdly, TDR contradicts the essence of PLUS: increased public management of growth. If property owners receive TDR that they can freely exchange, the county in effect relinquishes control over the location, density, and timing of future land use. TDR transactions could negate the comprehensive plan, CIP, APF ordinance, and EIS by changing the allocation of land uses they envision. Alternatively, if the county chooses to emphasize these latter measures, it would restrict the redistribution of TDR to the extent of overriding market mechanisms and stripping the program of significance.

This second alternative is likely since the county would hardly permit a developer to purchase enough rights to construct housing in excess of public facilities and services at a time when no new development was planned for the site. Thus not only do TDR impose rigid bounds and dependence on uncertain projection on public action, but they also allocate public decisionmaking responsibility to the private sector in contravention of PLUS's foundation.

Finally, the high cost of land makes land banking impractical. The Board of Supervisors allocated two million dollars of general revenue sharing funds in 1973 to establish a land bank.[115] This sum is so minute given the inflated value of land in the county, that it cannot possibly have a significant impact on local land use. Furthermore, the local government may actually increase land costs by entering the market for certain parcels, increasing demand, and causing prices to rise.

Indirect measures, such as fiscal constraints and incentives, appear to be more effective alternatives to public participation in the private marketplace. Reliance on tax policies would assure the county general and flexible authority that land banking cannot provide. It would also protect the government against adverse market conditions, such as fluctuations in land values and interest rates. Finally, fiscal controls would furnish tax revenues that the county could not collect on property it owned.

Thus the feasibility of implementing TDR and land banking is questionable, due to the legal and practical problems they create. Moreover the existence of preferable alternatives, such as comprehensive planning, capital improvements programming, and fiscal regulation, argue against these two controls. For these reasons, it is suggested that the PLUS directorate delete TDR and land banking from the work program. The funds set aside for a land bank could be applied to land acquisition for public purposes. To be successful, PLUS must contain compatible elements that achieve objectives in the most effective manner. TDR and land banking would detract from the substance of PLUS and should therefore not be pursued.

Conclusion

This analysis of PLUS programs indicates basic soundness, the need for modifications in some programs and serious deficiencies that warrant dropping others. The operational foundation of PLUS—comprehensive and development-oriented plans, CIP, APF and EIS ordinances—combines the most effective regulatory measures presently in use across the nation. Citizen participation and analytical tool development provide the cement that reinforces this foundation. Nevertheless, these programs contain flaws that should be remedied. Most of the recommendations, summarized below, involve administrative simplicity, methodological practicality, and philosophical consistency.

To provide citizen participation with organizational cohesion, it is suggested that increased emphasis be placed on the Planning Commission and EQAC. As a means of clarifying the role of analytical tool development, this program should be deferred until the comprehensive plan and CIP are adopted.

As a means of ensuring goal-oriented policy refinement and deterring physical determinism, it is proposed that the plans be reviewed in light of the PLUS policies and that the CIP be evaluated on the basis of adopted plans. To streamline operations, it is suggested that the countywide and district plans and the APF and EIS laws, respectively, be merged.

To avoid unreliable projections and retain governmental flexibility, it is proposed that TDR and land banking be deleted from PLUS. As a means of strengthening and safeguarding the active management of growth that PLUS embodies, it is recommended that the zoning ordinance and interim development controls be abandoned.

These proposals derive from a stronger concern for PLUS policies and implementation than the PLUS directorate presently exhibits. The current emphasis on program development is short-sighted and potentially harmful to PLUS. As the above criticisms of PLUS policies and programs demonstrate, the three processes of policymaking, program development, and implementation inextricably interact. By neglecting implementation during the program development phase, the PLUS leadership is developing elements that are incompatible, wasteful, and contradictory in some cases. A more balanced frame of reference would promote the unified and efficient operation that is vital to accomplish the PLUS goals.

10 The Planning and Land Use System: Implementation

Introduction

In the preceding three chapters, goals, policies, and programs adopted by Fairfax County were reviewed, and modifications of existing and proposed operations were recommended. This approach cannot be applied to PLUS implementation, because governmental plans are largely preliminary, fragmentary, and confidential. Whereas PLUS policies and programs were delineated to initiate staff work and permit public scrutiny and discussion, the administrative apparatus necessary to carry them out has yet to be unveiled.

Since governmental proposals are not completed and available for evaluation, an independent assessment of administrative requirements for PLUS implementation will be made. To perform this assessment, a strategy for bureaucratic innovation will be devised and applied to Fairfax County. This strategy focuses on the basic components of an administrative apparatus: functions, structure, and personnel. Its fundamental premise is that long-range planning for bureaucratic innovation must precede and guide interim measures. Therefore, the outcome of the analysis will be two-fold: an eventual administrative apparatus for PLUS implementation and temporary modifications that provide a transition from existing to proposed arrangements.

The recommendations will deal with the following governmental entities: Board of Supervisors, PC, EQAC, OCP, ORS, OEA, OMB, DPW and DCD, and BZA.

This strategy repudiates current management of implementation. Before detailing its contents, the basic flaws in county operations and their contributing causes will be identified.

Official Neglect of Implementation

Implementation encompasses two stages that are currently separate within PLUS, but which must overlap: administration of program development and of the final programs. Program development should be viewed as an integral yet interim phase of implementation, in other words, as an end and a means. Presently, the PLUS directorate is treating program development as an isolated, static end, except unintentionally for the OCP, whose interim and long-range administrative operations are virtually identical. This approach hinders implementation by robbing it of the second contribution program development should make.

For program development to provide a transition between previous and anticipated administrative activities, the PLUS leadership must determine its ultimate objectives in order to devise appropriate measures that promote them. The current gap between them, evident in the slight attention paid to long-range implementation while the programs are being prepared, is a political tactic that undermines the professional strategy essential to PLUS's success.

Three features of program preparation during the first six months of PLUS can account for the noticeable lack of adequate emphasis on implementation that is not apparent because of the need for circumspection. The others demonstrate a general absence of interest, arising from the different delegation of administrative responsibility for program development and implementation.

First, rivalry between the OCP and ORS for basic control of PLUS may have kept discussion of implementation behind the scenes. Although many other agencies are competing for responsibility for PLUS, these two members of the directorate are most involved. The intensity of their competition can be seen in the two following facts. On the one hand, the OCP has undergone the most complete administrative reorganization of any county agency for program development. On the other hand, ORS is directly in charge of the most expensive PLUS component: analytical tool development.

Comprehensive Planning's and Research and Statistics' major operational stakes in PLUS sets the stage for a confrontation that occurs in program development. Thus analytical tool development is proceeding simultaneously with comprehensive plan and capital improvements program preparation. This schedule keeps the work of the two offices in tandem. Until they resolve their competition, with or without intervention by third parties, such as the Board of Supervisors or Office of the County Executive, proposals for implementation are likely to remain tentative and concealed.

Secondly, several agencies with major responsibility for program development will play a relatively minor part in implementation. The most striking cases of this diminished role are the Offices of the County Executive and County Attorney. These offices essentially perform staff functions, while PLUS consists of line operations. Therefore routine administration of PLUS will be conducted by agencies with particular expertise in the program area. The present short-range perspective that blocks out implementation may have been partly engendered by the program development responsibilities of these agencies. In addition, agencies such as the OCP have hired staff on a temporary basis until implementation begins. These temporary employees are less likely to stress the long-run situation than permanent staff.

Thirdly, the absence of interest in implementation may have resulted from the initial assignment of many PLUS programs to consultants. Only citizen participation, the comprehensive and district plans, CIP, and EIS ordinance were delegated directly to county staff. The Board of Supervisors, Community Liaison Branch of OCP, Planning Commission, and EQAC are the major governmental participants in citizen participation: the OCP in the comprehensive and district plans and CIP, and the Offices of Environmental Affairs and of the County Attorney in the EIS ordinance. Primary responsibility for the APF ordinance, interim development controls, land banking, and TDR was assigned to a land use law consultant and staff; the zoning ordinance to the ZOSC and a DCD consultant; and analytical tool development to systems analysis consultants.

Although staff assistance and/or supervision was provided for each program, the consultants established a restricted focus on their contractual obligations. And except for the land use law expert, who drew up plans for implementation, the consultants concentrated on program development. By and large, therefore, implementation was omitted from initial consultant work on PLUS. Since over half the programs were in their hands, the presence of temporary consultants may have impeded a staff effort to consider implementation.

Hence the initial division of labor for program development may have encouraged either apparent or real neglect of PLUS implementation, evident in early 1974. Three facets of program development—rivalry between the Offices of Comprehensive Planning and Research and Statistics, temporary roles of some PLUS staff, and consultant contracts—may have created the impression that interest in implementation is negligible. This impression must be dispelled by acute concern with implementation if Fairfax County wants to produce a cohesive system. Although disjointed programs may enhance the immediate political acceptability of PLUS, this advantage can result in administrative chaos when an attempt is made to carry out the programs.

It is contended that the administration of program development must accomplish an objective in addition to the primary assignment of preparing the PLUS components. It must set the stage for program implementation in a deliberate and open manner. An operational transition between pre-existing and anticipated land use regulation is essential. All administrative repercussions of PLUS, not merely its immediate demands, must be addressed. To pursue this ulterior objective, the following strategy for bureaucratic innovation is suggested.

A Strategy for Bureaucratic Innovation

Introduction

The strategy for bureaucratic innovation deals with a variation of governmental implementation. Most bureaucratic operations are routine and repetitive, but PLUS directs public attention on the extraordinary process of change. Like the more general implementation, innovation involves the three components of an administrative apparatus: functions, structure, and personnel. Peculiar to innovation, however, is the primary significance of the ways and extent to which these components can be modified.

Bureaucratic innovation thus has qualitative and quantitative aspects, the former relating to the administrative components and the latter to the intensity of change. On the one hand, functions, structure, and personnel can be manipulated, either singly or together. The instigators of change may be constrained in the degree to which they can separate the components from each other. For example, a functional modification might necessitate concommitant adjustments in organization staff. But regardless of the limits imposed by external circumstances, change involves one or several of the components.

On the other hand, the intensity of change can be varied. Intensity has both magnitude and range. Magnitude can be conceived as a continuum ranging from expansion to replacement. At each extreme, functions, structure, and staff can be added or substituted in the existing administrative apparatus. Within these limits, an infinite number of permutations and combinations involving addition and/or substitution of aspects of three components are possible. To simplify the analysis, the range of options available to the PLUS directorate will be restricted to these two extremes.

Range refers to the rapidity with which change takes place. It may often be possible to subdivide a major innovation into discrete steps that can be accomplished individually. Thus the time required to bring about change also can be controlled.

The form that these qualitative and quantitative aspects of bureaucratic innovation assume in Fairfax County depends on specific conditions. This strategy thus requires establishing an empirical frame of reference in order to determine the appropriate type and intensity of change that should be achieved.

The strategy for managing governmental change contains assumptions, objectives, and methods. The assumptions are universal, whereas the objectives and methods must be tailored to local circumstances in Fairfax County. This strategy is intended to facilitate optimal bureaucratic innovation. Its usefulness as a guide for PLUS implementation will be tested in the following analysis.

Assumptions

Four assumptions regarding the nature of bureaucratic change provide a foundation for the strategy. The first and second complement each other, as do the third and fourth.

The first and second assumptions are that bureaucratic change is controllable and conservative. On the one hand, various participants in the political system described in Part I can determine its form and impact. The administrative apparatus is understandable and governable, yet not entirely predictable due to the complexity of the political system, particularly the diffusion of authority. Because elected, appointed, and career officials are somewhat autonomous and subject to extra-governmental influence, none can dictate bureaucratic change.

On the other hand, since authority is shared, the system is responsive to all participants, although not necessarily to the same extent or in a consistent manner. In any case, no single participant is omniscient or omnipotent, and cooperation is therefore essential. Thus governmental innovation takes place within the existing political context and proceeds through negotiation, bargaining, and compromise. Given the controllable and conservative characteristics of bureaucratic change, these means are both available and vital.

Thirdly, governmental innovation contains an element of the zero-sum game. Over the long run, change will benefit some individuals or agencies at the expense of others. Isolated modifications need not produce immediate positive and negative results, yet when considered cumulatively they have this divergent impact.

Change is interpreted differently by those it affects, based on their perceptions of the eventual administrative outcome. In varying degrees, change is viewed as either advantageous or disadvantageous to them. These perceived ramifications are themselves subject to revision in light of changing circumstances.

Fourthly, resistance to change is inevitable in a political system where authority is divided among diverse individuals and entities. Modifications produce winners and losers. State enabling legislation, civil service regulations, seniority, technical expertise, and public sentiment all sanction the exercise of power by various members of the government. These forms of allegiance shift their focus with changing circumstances, but authority always retains a broad distribution.

The diffusion of responsibility and differential impact of modifications require initiators of change to anticipate and respond to resistance. They must consider negative repercussions of bureaucratic innovation and mitigate them to the greatest extent feasible. If the modifications are either urgent or modest enough to furnish support that can override opposition and at least permit some implementation, then they should be undertaken. On the other hand, if resistance that can undermine the innovations and perhaps the position of its proponents is expected, they should not be instituted at that time. In other words, only change that will probably yield net positive results, either in the short run or long run, is worthwhile.

Objectives

Since all segments of the bureaucracy exert some influence over public business and resistance to innovation is a foregone conclusion, the least disruptive course of action that achieves the desired end should be pursued. This approach embodies two objectives: moderation and effectiveness.

Based on the above description of qualitative and quantitative bureaucratic innovation, moderate change entails a single administrative component rather than several, addition rather than replacement, and longer rather than shorter time span. When all three preferable alternatives occur, moderation is maximized. Often, however, circumstances prevent this outcome, and the initiators of change must seek the closest approximation of this objective.

Complementing moderation as an objective of this strategy for bureaucratic innovation is effectiveness. In this context, effectiveness denotes the maximum gain or minimum loss resulting from a type and intensity of change. This gain or loss is the net expected outcome obtained by weighing the benefit of an innovation against the disruption it causes in the existing administrative machinery.

Two measures of administrative effectiveness will be applied to an evaluation: fragmentation and counterproductivity. Fragmentation refers to an excessive division of labor, namely the use of more functions, staff, and/or organization than are necessary to accomplish a task. This measure includes overlapping and duplicated activities. Counterproductivity refers to conflicting or extraneous personnel, structure, and/or procedures. A counterproductive bureaucratic innovation yields operations that lack coordination or coherence.

A comparison of the broad objectives—moderation and effectiveness—reveals potential conflict. The more gradual an innovation, the more likely it is to fragment or contradict the existing administrative machinery. On the contrary, the more effective a modification, the more likely it is to replace a previous arrangement and thus be more disruptive. While tension is inevitable, it is also resolvable. Because to some extent moderation and effectiveness intrinsically diverge, a strategy for managing governmental change by mediating between them must be formulated. Since government runs through bargaining and negotiation, they can be pursued simultaneously, each counterbalancing the other. As will be demonstrated, compromises that are workable, though not quite satisfactory to all parties, result.

Methodology

Managing bureaucratic innovation so as to balance the sometimes incongruous objectives of moderation and effectiveness requires three steps. First an assessment of the current governmental apparatus for land use regulation must be made. This step involves a review of the PLUS program and other land use regulatory activities, namely in the Departments of County Development and Public Works. Administrative aspects of PLUS were introduced in the preceding appraisal of program development. These aspects will be integrated into the discussion of existing operations.

Secondly, the ultimate administrative apparatus must be established, also with reference to PLUS and other development controls. The essence of these long-range implementation mechanisms is embodied in the above recommendations for improving the PLUS program. To achieve the suggested consolidations and deletions requires modifications in governmental functions, structure, and staff.

These long-range plans constitute parameters for interim measures—the third step. Depending on the type and intensity of the changes envisioned, they may be pursued in their entirety immediately, or at a future time subdivided into discrete parts, and accomplished gradually.

However, application of this three-step methodology to Fairfax County requires an adjustment in the process of selecting long-range and then short-range administrative alternations. Various bureaucratic innovations were instituted in 1973 to expedite PLUS program development. Thus some short-range changes have preceded long-range planning. These interim administrative modifications will be taken into consideration in formulating the eventual apparatus, and an attempt will be made to retain them where they promote moderation and effectiveness.

**An Administrative Apparatus for
PLUS Implementation: Application of
the Strategy**

Introduction

The strategy for bureaucratic innovation will be applied in order to derive an administrative apparatus for PLUS implementation. The analysis of present, ultimate, and interim functions, organization, and personnel will consist of two parts.

First, county land use control activities will be assessed using the three-step methodology. This evaluation will encompass PLUS programs, as modified in the preceding section, and relevant County Development and Public Works operations. The specific program areas are: citizen participation, analytical tool development, planning, capital improvements programming, zoning, public works and facilities regulation, and EI/PF ordinance administration. The earlier recommendations for program development set guidelines for the ultimate administrative apparatus, since changes in program contents have ramifications for functions, structure, and staff. Administrative aspects of these proposals will be elaborated, and pre-existing development regulatory devices will be incorporated in the appraisal.

A recent board action affects present functions in three program areas: citizen participation, zoning, and development. On 4 March 1974 the supervisors imposed a development ban that prohibited granting new rezonings, building or sewer permits with a few exceptions.[116] Contrary to the sub-local moratoria proposed in the interim development controls program, this ban is countrywide. It has been challenged by developers in public hearings and in the courts. Whether or not it is upheld, for the present it has drastically altered the operations of the Board of Supervisors, PC, and the Zoning Administration, Design Review, and Inspections Branches of the DCD.

These entities all participate in the review of rezoning applications, project proposals, and other stages of the development process. The ban has not curtailed the activities of the board or the PC, which are heavily involved in PLUS. However, it has left many County Development staff members virtually idle. Their situation will be noted in the analysis.

Secondly, the current, eventual, and transitional functions, structure, and personnel will be summarized within the context of county agencies. The proposed administrative machinery for PLUS implementation will focus on those governmental entities that play a primary role in PLUS or are significantly affected by it. Consequently, bureaucratic innovations will be suggested for the following: Board of Supervisors, PC, EQAC, BZA, OCP, ORS, OMB, OEA, DCD, and DPW. Organizational charts will be provided to pinpoint the suggested modifications.

Before delineating administrative changes from the program perspective, specific constraints on the application of the strategy's objectives should be noted. With respect to effectiveness, most of the PLUS programs comprise activities that duplicate, overlap with, or contradict other PLUS programs or pre-existing land use regulatory activities. The bulk of the proposed innovations will deal with this objective, since it has been largely disregarded.

In reference to moderation, the PLUS timetable has predetermined the duration of the interim period. Although some of the PLUS programs are behind schedule and the exact completion date is therefore uncertain, it will be assumed that all temporary modifications will end in the summer of 1975. Also, relating to moderation in personnel changes, it will not be possible to specify whether temporary staff will finish their assignments and leave the county as pre-arranged, or permanent staff must be phased out. This distinction cannot be made because records of which new staff members were hired in temporary positions are confidential.

Citizen Participation

Citizen participation has distinct structural and staffing elements, but its current functional element—review of the PLUS components—overlaps with all the other programs. In evaluating its functional element, the overlapping will be understood and thus will not be reiterated in each case.

To accomplish its present function, citizen participation utilizes district and countywide forums, special groups, PC, Board of Supervisors and EQAC meetings, and Community Liaison Branch operations. As mentioned earlier, present activities are ineffective due to duplication and fragmentation and the ambiguous role of the PC and EQAC. In addition, there is inadequate coordination between the OCP staff and advisory bodies.

In the long run, it is proposed that citizen participation encompass evaluation of development proposals from the standpoint of plans and the EI/PF ordinance and also review of updated comprehensive plans and capital improvements programs. The organization and personnel corresponding to these functions would be the PC, EQAC, Board of Supervisors, and Community Liaison Branch.

The Board of Supervisors would participate in all these activities. To perpetuate its expanded commitment to citizen participation initiated with PLUS, two major changes in board procedures are suggested. First, the board should reserve one week of each month for two evening sessions dealing with land use regulation, rather than one day-long session. Since many county residents work, they are unable to attend daytime hearings. To ensure maximum community involvement in growth management, this week of evening sessions should be furnished. Secondly, when the board conducts hearings on district planning elements, meetings should be held in the district under consideration. Decentralized operations would facilitate attendance by citizens most directly affected by the proposed plans.

The PC would be responsible for applying the plans and the EQAC, the EI/PF law to proposed developments. To promote closer staff/advisory body coordination, it is recommended that the chief of the Community Liaison Branch replace the at-large member of the PC. The Virginia code provides for one agency official to sit on this advisory body, and thus no special enabling legislation is needed.[117] To function effectively, the PC should remain at its present size and contain an odd number of members. For these reasons, the OCP staff member is not simply added to the advisory body.

Citizen participation's eventual administrative apparatus would differ from its present one in three respects. First, the forums and groups established for PLUS program development would be discontinued. Secondly, the Community Liaison staff would be smaller, since citizen participation would be channeled primarily through the Board of Supervisors, PC and EQAC. Finally, the PC and EQAC would have more restricted roles. Instead of assessing all aspects of PLUS, they would each have one major program area.

Three interim measures are suggested to afford transition between these present and ultimate administrative mechanisms. First, the committee structure based on geographical representation in the BOS, PC, and EQAC, which was proposed in the evaluation of citizen participation, should be instituted. Secondly, the Community Liaison Branch chief should be appointed to the PC. He would serve as a non-voting representative with the nine present members for the time being. When the term of the at-large number expires, the vacancy would not be filled. The OCP branch chief would thereby replace this member and participate fully in commission proceedings. Finally, the size of the Community Liaison Branch should be reduced, either through attrition, completion of temporary assignments, or termination of permanent staff.

Analytical Tool Development

In keeping with the anti-modeling bias of many officials and citizens, analytical tool development has been scaled down to surveys, specific computerized information, and other limited tasks, such as improving the capabilities of the UDIS. OCP and ORS competition for control of the program persists, and both agencies have personnel assigned to it. Additional staff were hired in the Management Statistics Branch of the ORS to monitor PLUS in connection with the program. One of the designated functions of the Technical Studies Branch, formed during the Office of Comprehensive Planning's reorganization of mid-1973, was to handle data analysis. Consultants working primarily with the Technical Studies Branch constitute some of the program staff at present.

Over the long run, it is recommended that the program's products—a revamped UDIS and other data banks—be managed by the Technical Studies Branch. This ultimate administrative apparatus requires two major modifications in present operations. First, as the consultant role ends, monitoring and updating will replace analytical tool development as the primary functions. Secondly, responsibility will shift from the ORS, which performs most of the county systems analysis, to the OCP, where the information is most needed.

To provide a transition from current to anticipated functions, structure, and staff, two interim measures are proposed. First, the Research Branch of ORS, which manages UDIS, should be abolished. Some of its staff would be incorporated in the Technical Studies Branch, where they would continue their previous work. Secondly, the staff of the Management Statistics and Technical Studies Branches should be cut back, due to the more limited responsibility of applying the analytical tools developed for PLUS.

Planning

The planning administrative apparatus includes the Comprehensive Plans Branch of OCP, which is preparing countywide and district plans, and the citizen participation machinery, which is evaluating them. Presently, consultants are conducting detailed studies of sub-areas within planning districts.[118] Comprehensive Plans Branch staff members have been assigned several planning districts and are handling both the countywide and district aspects. This arrangement contains two potential problems. On the one hand, the division between countywide and district plans may rob the former of flexibility and relevance. On the other hand, the use of district plans may perpetuate boundaries that are now anachronistic.

For the future, it is proposed that the Comprehensive Plans Branch, Board of Supervisors, and PC apply unified plans to development applications. Also, the Comprehensive Plans Branch will update plans, which will be reviewed by the other two bodies. There are three differences between these eventual and present administrative apparatuses. First, the countywide and district plans would be consolidated into a single plan. Secondly, the Comprehensive Plans Branch would be smaller. Finally, the BOS, PC, and staff would focus more on applying the plan than on drafting it.

To accomplish these anticipated operations, three interim steps are recommended. First, the functions of the Comprehensive Plans Branch should be regrouped. Personnel should be delegated functional and not geographical areas to integrate the countywide and district components. Either individual staff members or teams should deal with several subject areas. Secondly, planning district boundaries should be appraised. If they are found to be deficient, modifications should be made to improve their utility. Thirdly, staff must be cut. The consultants will automatically drop out of the program when their tasks are completed. In addition, some personnel must be terminated, since the branch's primary responsibility—plan application—represents a drastic curtailment of activity.

Capital Improvements Programming

Capital improvements programming involves the preparation of a five-year budget by the Public Facilities Branch of OCP, based on individual agency and OMB data. This function will be expanded to provide a twenty-year budget, after the comprehensive plan has been completed and standards and criteria have been established. Currently OMB and OCP overlap to some extent and are competing for authority over the CIP. Apart from this duplication, the lack of a plan and guidelines prevents long-range projections.

Eventually, the Public Facilities Branch will prepare and update capital improvements budgets. Unlike the other programs, whose ultimate administrative apparatuses will be operational when implementation begins, the CIP has encountered difficulties that will necessitate an extended program development phase. The conversion from annual to long-range capital facilities budgeting entails information and standards that are currently in preparation. Without a completed plan and criteria, the twenty-year projections envisioned in PLUS must be postponed. For these reasons, a five-year CIP is the immediate program objective, and the twenty-year version is expected after 1975.

This ultimate administrative arrangement requires two interim modifications in present operations. First, responsibility for the CIP must be transferred completely from the OMB to the OCP. A joint OCP/OMB task force on capital facilities should be established to coordinate their overlapping activities. Since the Public Facilities Branch will assume this function in the future, its chief should direct the task force.

Secondly, the Public Facilities Branch and OMB staff must be reduced. Fewer OCP personnel will be needed because the long-range budget would be completed, and only relatively limited updating will be performed. Less OMB staff work will be required, since capital facilities budgeting will no longer be an agency function. Some personnel from each office would have to be cut, unless attrition and/or departure of temporary staff furnishes sufficient vacancies.

Zoning

Due to the development ban, zoning activity is concentrated on the new ordinance, which is under review by the Board of Supervisors and PC. The ZOSC, working out of the DCD, has primary responsibility for the revised law. Operations of the Zoning Administration and Design Review Divisions of DCD and the BZA have dwindled in response to the lighter work load. The Technical Studies Branch of OCP collaborates with the Design Review Division to prepare the staff report on rezoning applications. Its PLUS activities have kept staff fully occupied despite the development ban. When the new zoning ordinance is enacted, DCD personnel will reclassify all county land in accordance with the revised system.

Zoning is an inferior and obsolescent land use control that is potentially detrimental to PLUS. Since it cannot make a positive contribution and may impede implementation, zoning should be abolished in the long run. This recommendation necessitates dismantling the current zoning administration machinery.

Three specific changes must be made to eliminate zoning. First, the Zoning Administration Division of DCD and, secondly, the BZA will cease operations. These entities deal exclusively with zoning and will therefore serve no useful purpose. Thirdly, the Board of Supervisors, PC, and OCP and DCD staff will discontinue their zoning-related activities: hearings on proposed rezonings, staff reports, and presentations. The EI/PF ordinance will replace the zoning ordinance as the focus of land use regulation.

To achieve this ultimate outcome, four interim measures are suggested. First, the new zoning ordinance and all associated administrative activities should be abandoned. Even if zoning operations continue, they should be based on the old law. Since zoning will be phased out, the effort that adoption of the new ordinance involves is not warranted.

Secondly, most of the Zoning Administration Division staff should be transferred to the OCP, which will have major responsibility for administering the EI/PF ordinance. Some personnel in this DCD branch should be retained to handle existing and incoming rezoning applications. Also, if implementation of the EI/PF ordinance is delayed by lawsuits or an unfavorable judicial ruling, the county will have to rely on zoning to regulate development.

Thirdly, it is proposed that the Zoning Administration Division personnel relocated in the OCP reclassify the parcels in the zoning files according to guidelines set for the EI/PF ordinance. In other words, environmental and public facilities and services features of the parcels should be identified to expedite the replacement of zoning by the innovative land use control. Following this conversion, some of the DCD staff members should be terminated, since the processing of new development requests will represent a diminished work load.

Finally, the Zoning Administration Division and the BZA should be abolished. The timing of this measure depends on the fate of the EI/PF law. Zoning operations must continue until they can be replaced to ensure some local control over land use. After the EI/PF ordinance takes effect, zoning should be eliminated.

Public Works and Facilities Regulation

Complementing zoning, the initial stage in the land use process is public works and facilities regulation, which currently is divided administratively along public and private lines. The DPW handles the infrastructure that the county furnishes to all land uses, such as sewers and roads, and also public facilities. The DCD deals with private residential, commercial, and industrial facilities, including the infrastructure they require. This arrangement fragments land use control through duplicated functions, structure and personnel. Specifically, the Maintenance and Construction and Projects Engineering Divisions of DPW overlap respectively with the Inspections and Design Review Divisions of DCD.

In the long run, it is proposed that the DPW perform engineering, maintenance, construction, and inspections services for public and private land use infrastructure. Additionally, this agency will be responsible for the design of public facilities.

This ultimate administrative apparatus represents the dismantling of the DCD and integration of its Inspections Division into the DPW. A complete merger of the two agencies is not suggested, because the private land use regulation previously conducted by DCD will be either discontinued or transferred to OCP.

Four interim measures are proposed to ease the transition from current to eventual operations. First, the Mapping Division of the DCD should be transferred to the OCP. This branch should combine with the planning library to form a new OCP Reference Branch. All original staff should be retained, since they do not currently overlap and their work loads are expected to remain at present levels.

Secondly, the Administrative Services Division of the DCD should be abolished, as the two agencies that will subsume remaining DCD activities—OCP and DPW—have adequate administrative support.

Thirdly, the Design Review Division of the DCD should be abolished, since the EI/PF ordinance will encompass its functions. A Development Regulation Branch will be proposed for the OCP to administer this ordinance. Some Design Review staff members may be included in this new branch. Personnel cuts will be required, however, because the PLUS commitment to limit growth will reduce the amount of future development and therefore necessitate less staff.

Fourth, the Inspections Division of the DCD should be combined with the Maintenance and Construction Division of DPW to form a temporary joint section located in the DPW. Both staff would be retained intact while a unified data bank and set of guidelines and procedures are prepared. Following the functional merger of these units, staff would be reduced because of duplication and diminished work load expected with tighter development controls. Structurally, the joint section would revert back to the original Public Works division: Maintenance and Construction.

Environmental Impact/Public
Facilities Ordinance Administration

At present the administrative apparatus for the EIS and APF ordinances consists of Environmental Affairs Office personnel for the former and OCP, and ORS, and DCD personnel and consultants for the latter. Since neither law has been completed, functions and organization have not been established. As discussed in the preceding section, adequacy of public facilities is a type of environmental impact. It was contended, therefore, that the current separate pieces of legislation should be combined into a single EI/PF ordinance.

Eventually, the EI/PF ordinance will replace the zoning ordinance as the primary land use control in Fairfax County. Instead of submitting a rezoning application and then site plans and plats, developers will prepare a development application that includes an EIS and survey of public facilities relating to their proposal. Following staff analysis, the development application will be reviewed by the PC for conformity with county plans and by the EQAC for adherence to the criteria in the EI/PF ordinance. The final decision of whether to grant or deny the application will be made by the Board of Supervisors.

In accordance with this conversion, a Development Regulation Branch will be created in the OCP, which in light of its expanded functions, will be renamed the Department of Planning and Land Use Control (DPLUC). This branch will be staffed by former OEA, Public Facilities, Technical Studies, and Design Review personnel.

To arrange this ultimate administrative apparatus, four interim measures are proposed. First, the EIS and APF ordinances should be consolidated into a law covering both. The Technical Studies Branch would take responsibility for enforcing the EI/PF ordinance.

Secondly, the OEA should be abolished and its staff integrated into the newly formed DPLUC. OEA served primarily as staff to EQAC. With the more restricted role anticipated for this advisory body, this function can be eliminated. The director of OEA would become chief of the Development Regulation Branch. Other OEA personnel would also be incorporated in this branch, joining the Design Review and Zoning Administration staff. To prepare for administering the EI/PF ordinance, this staff would determine and apply environmental and public facilities criteria to the zoning files. After this assignment is completed, staff reductions would occur to compensate for the smaller work load.

Thirdly, the County Development and Research and Statistics staff working on the APF ordinance and some Environmental Affairs staff involved with the EIS ordinance should be transferred temporarily to the OCP Technical Studies Branch. This personnel would continue to prepare the merged ordinance under centralized direction. Following the completion of the law, most staff responsible for its formulation would be cut from the Technical Studies Branch. Some personnel might be reassigned to the Development Regulation Branch or ORS, and others would be terminated.

Finally, administration of the EI/PF ordinance will require expertise possessed by Technical Studies and Public Facilities personnel. Therefore, several staff members from these branches, whose work load would diminish after program development ends, should be transferred to the Development Regulation Branch. This branch would thus eventually contain personnel from OEA, DCD, Public Facilities, and Technical Studies.

Recapitulation

In order to highlight the major administrative features envisioned for PLUS implementation, the new functions, structure, and personnel of the affected agencies will be summarized. Figure 10-1 and Figure 10-2 indicate the existing and ultimate outcomes, respectively.

Board of Supervisors. The Board of Supervisors will maintain the same structure and staff and will modify its functions in three respects: decentralized hearings on district planning components, substitution of two evening sessions for one daily session per month; and replacement of zoning-related activities by EI/PF ordinance administration.

Planning Commission. The PC will replace its at-large member by the Community Liaison Branch chief and substitute review of development proposals for conformity with county plans for zoning-related operations.

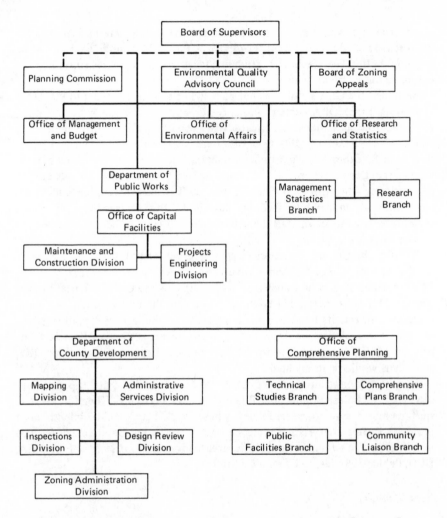

Figure 10-1. Partial Structure of Current Agencies with Primary Involvement in PLUS.

Environmental Quality Advisory Council. The EQAC will review development proposals for adherence to EI/PF ordinance guidelines.

Board of Zoning Appeals. The BZA will be abolished.

Office of Environmental Affairs. The OEA will be dismantled and its staff transferred to the DPLUC or terminated.

Office of Research and Statistics. The Research Branch of the ORS will be dismantled and its staff and functions transferred to the Technical Studies

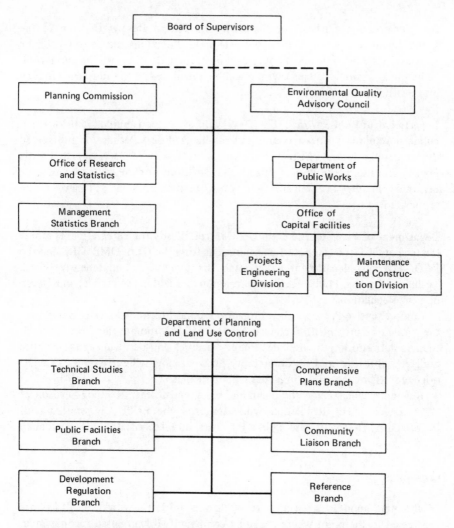

Figure 10-2. Partial Structure of Proposed Agencies with Primary Involvement in PLUS.

Branch of the DPLUC. In addition, some personnel hired in the Management Statistics Branch for analytical tool development will be cut.

Office of Management and Budget. The OMB will transfer all capital facilities budgeting to the Public Facilities Branch of the DPLUC and cut back on staff to compensate for fewer functions.

Department of County Development. The DCD will be abolished and some of its staff transferred to other agencies: Inspections Division to the Maintenance and Construction Division in the DPW and Design Review Division to the Development Regulation Branch of the DPLUC. Functions and personnel of the Administrative Services and Zoning Administration Divisions will be eliminated, while those of the Mapping Division will be transferred to the Reference Branch of the DPLUC.

Department of Public Works. The DPW will have responsibility for private and public development infrastructure and public facilities. Because of anticipated slower growth under PLUS, no additional staff will be necessary to handle private land use in the Project Engineering Division. For the same reason, some personnel in the Maintenance and Construction Division will have to be terminated.

Department of Planning and Land Use Control. Lastly the DPLUC will combine the former OCP and some staff and functions from the OEA, OMB, ORS and the DCD. The new department will contain six branches: Comprehensive Plans, Technical Studies, Public Facilities, Community Liaison, Reference, and Development Regulation.

Comprehensive Plans will be reorganized along functional lines to administer the unified county plan. Technical Studies will incorporate the ORS Research Branch staff and improved UDIS. Public Facilities will perform capital facilities budgeting through the CIP. Community Liaison's chief will serve on the PC. The original staffs of these four branches will be smaller.

Reference will include the planning library and former Mapping Division of DCD. Development Regulation will administer the EI/PF law, staffed with former OEA, Design Review, Public Facilities, and Technical Studies personnel.

Conclusion

In the nine months since this research was initiated, work on PLUS has progressed to the point where it can be compared with proposed recommendations. This study took the original proposals for PLUS and early county activities and derived an optimal political and administrative scenario. Now that PLUS has established a tangible foundation, it is appropriate to build upon it in the conclusion. Therefore, this discussion will summarize actual county efforts with respect to the following: the governmental perspective on land use control, local leadership, board/staff/advisory body relations, and implementation of the PLUS programs.

A perspective that encompasses local, regional, state, and federal participants was proposed in light of the political system within which Fairfax County operates. At the local level, the housing industry in particular was stressed. The county has embraced some of this perspective, but not all of it.

Fairfax's frame of reference is, with one exception, exclusively local. The board and senior administrative staff in the PLUS directorate have concentrated on county residents and employees. Community involvement and staff activities are the present pillars of PLUS. On the other hand, local developers, neighboring jurisdictions, and the state government are excluded from the mainstream of public action.

The exception to this local focus is contact with the federal government. However, the motivation for this contact is apprehension about state intervention in county affairs. Thus it too is symptomatic of overriding concern with the locality. In early 1974, a delegation of staff members met with officials in the Interior Department's Office of Land Use and Water Planning, charged with administering the national land use policy legislation. Their intention was to explain PLUS as a means of convincing these federal officials to accord localities broad discretion in planning and land use control. Fearful that the conservative Virginia legislature would veto innovative measures, they sought to demonstrate local capabilities through their achievements.

A definition of leadership combining the ability to act and inspire was postulated for the board acting under PLUS. Two indicators of its ability to lead were described: legitimization and policy refinement. The board has met the two criteria in their steps to legitimize PLUS, but not in their policymaking activities.

On the positive side, the board followed up on its adoption of PLUS by generating popular support and involvement and delegating administrative responsibility for implementation to staff. On the negative side, the interim development and redevelopment policies have not been translated into objectives and standards for staff. The major policy that the board promulgated was the development ban, which prohibits most new growth until PLUS's regulatory tools are completed.

This juxtaposition between leadership with respect to legitimization, but not policy refinement may be less than fortuitous. The board has built a local consensus on PLUS, cemented by commitment to managed growth. The citizens and community groups that comprise this consensus advocate strong public controls over developers. Their unity, however, does not extend to the unresolved issues implicit in the policy statement. Therefore, perhaps to retain its broad political base, the board is neither initiating policy refinement nor encouraging staff to perform the task.

Conflict observed between the supervisors operating through the advisory bodies, and staff, impeding board action, has diminished under PLUS. Since public involvement is a basic feature of PLUS, competition among the board, bureaucracy, and counterbureaucracy is minimized. Responsiveness and efficiency are not only compatible, they also complement each other.

Essentially, the board appears satisfied to emphasize responsiveness and allow staff to pursue efficiency. Its major accomplishments are the countywide and district forums and other citizen participation measures and the development ban. The staff's contribution has revolved around the following components: comprehensive and district plans, CIP, EIS and APF ordinances, land use control improvement program, analytical tool development, and converging with the supervisors, citizen participation.

In the substantive and administrative recommendations for PLUS, the assumption that innovative techniques should replace existing regulatory mechanisms was made. Thus the abolition of zoning, merger of comprehensive and district plans, and alternate administrative apparatus were proposed. It is now evident that the county's approach consists of grafting new and old components to form an improved system for managing growth. The zoning, EIS and APF ordinances, and the countywide and district plans, respectively, are intended to coexist. PLUS therefore has a conservative orientation, since it retains traditional regulatory mechanisms while adopting innovative techniques.

PLUS is conservative in another significant respect: its eclecticism. With reference to land use controls that are novel for Virginia, each has precedents in other states or localities. For example, California requires an environmental impact statement for coastal development and Ramapo, New York enacted an adequate public facilities ordinance. Although these precedents are not legally binding in Virginia, they provide compelling support for Fairfax County's own EIS and APF laws.

Counterbalancing this conservatism is the fundamental originality of PLUS. Developing a system that entails wholesale governmental reorientation is unique. Whether this extraordinary endeavor will succeed remains to be determined. Regardless of the outcome, the ambitiousness that PLUS embodies is commendable.

The Department of Housing and Urban Development recently awarded a grant to the Urban Institute to monitor PLUS and prepare a handbook for local governments based on Fairfax's experience. This Federal interest is a sign that PLUS has the potential to influence local management of growth across the nation. The recognition that this project represents is deserved in view of the effort that the county is making. It can only be hoped that PLUS will fulfill these expectations.

Notes

Notes

1. Interview with Mr. E.A. Prichard, attorney, Boothe, Prichard and Dudley, and former councilman and mayor of the city of Fairfax, in the city of Fairfax, Va., on August 17, 1973.

2. Interview with William P. Croom III, executive vice-president, Northern Virginia Builders Association, in McLean, Va., on September 20, 1973.

3. Interview with Mr. Prichard.

4. U.S. Bureau of the Census, *Census of Population 1950, 1960, 1970, General Population Characteristics*, Virginia, PC(1)-B.

5. *Five Year Countywide Development Program: Presentation of Alternatives*, vol. 1 (Fairfax County, August 7, 1972), p. xiii.

6. Ibid., p. 18.

7. U.S. Bureau of the Census, *Census of Population 1960*, Virginia, PC(1)-48D.

8. U.S. Bureau of the Census, *Census of Population and Housing 1970*, Washington, D.C.-Md.-Va. SMSA, PHC(1)-226.

9. U.S. Bureau of the Census, *Census of Population 1960 and 1970*, Virginia, PC(1)-48C.

10. Ibid.

11. Ibid. and Office of Research and Statistics, Fairfax County, 1973.

12. *Five Year Countywide Development Program*, p. 42.

13. U.S. Bureau of the Census, *Census of Housing 1960 and 1970*, Virginia, HC(1).

14. Ibid.

15. Department of Assessments, Fairfax County, 1972.

16. Population Reference Bureau, "Suburban Growth: A Case Study," *Population Bulletin*, vol. 28, no. 1 (Washington, 1972), p. 5.

17. *1960 Annual Report* (Fairfax County, 1961) p. 11; *The Citizen's Handbook and Annual Report, FY 72*, (Fairfax County, January 1973), p. 52.

18. John L. Hysom, Jr. "An Evaluation of the Effects of the Planning and Zoning Criteria Used for Allocating Land for Residential Purposes in Fairfax County, Virginia" (doctoral dissertation, The American University, second draft, May 15, 1973) pp. 231-2.

19. Traffic and Safety Division, Virginia Department of Highways, *Average Daily Traffic Volumes on Interstate, Arterial, and Primary Routes, 1962-63* (Richmond, 1963), pp. 112; Idem, *Average Daily Traffic Volumes on Interstate, Arterial and Primary Routes, 1972* (Richmond, 1973), p. 145.

20. Traffic and Safety Division, Virginia Department of Highways, *Average Daily Traffic, 1962-3*, p. 112; Idem, *Average Daily Traffic, 1972*, p. 145.

21. *Five Year Countywide Development Program*, p. 107.

22. Ibid., p. 107.

23. Interview with Mr. Prichard.

24. Population Reference Bureau, p. 22

25. *Code of Virginia*, chap. 15, Title 15.1-765.

26. Ibid., Title 15.1-779.

27. Ibid., chap. 11, Title 15.1-493 and 494.

28. *The Citizen's Handbook and Annual Report*, p. 3.

29. Office of Research and Statistics, "Techniques for Improving Board Procedures with Special Attention to Administrative Procedures," (Fairfax County, September 1973), p. 5.

30. Interview with Donald R. Bowman, director, Office of Environmental Affairs and former member of the Board of Supervisors, Fairfax County, in the city of Fairfax, Va., on July 24, 1973.

31. Code of Virginia, chap. 14, Title 14.1-46.

32. Cresap, McCormick and Paget, "Fairfax County Management Audit of the County Government Organization and Operation: Preliminary Recommendations." 1968, pp. II-1, II-6.

33. *1967 Annual Report*, (Fairfax County, 1968), p. 3; *1968 Annual Report*, (Fairfax County, 1969), p. 3; *1969 Annual Report*, (Fairfax County, 1970), pp. 37 and 42.

34. "Proposed Department of County Development," (Fairfax County, 1968), p. 5.

35. *1967 Annual Report*, p. 3; *1968 Annual Report*, p. 3.

36. *The Citizen's Handbook and Annual Report*, pp. 4-5.

37. *Washington Post*, Feb. 8, 1972.

38. *1962 Annual Report*, (Fairfax County, 1963), p. 3; *1966 Annual Report*, (Fairfax County, 1967), p. 3; *1967 Annual Report*, (Fairfax County, 1968), p. 5; *1969 Annual Report*, (Fairfax County, 1970), p. 5.

39. *Washington Post*, Feb. 8, 1972.

40. Hysom, p. 121.

41. Ibid., pp. 139 and 180.

42. Interview with William P. Croom III, executive vice-president, Northern Virginia Builders Association, in McLean, Va., on September 20, 1973.

43. Hysom, p. 66.

44. Ibid., p. 62.

45. Ibid., pp. 85-6.

46. Ibid., pp. 43-4.

47. Ibid., p. 68.

48. Ibid., p. 54.

49. Ibid., pp. 95-7.

50. Ibid., p. 186.

51. Interview with James C. Wyckoff, administrative assistant to the Fairfax County Planning Commission, in the city of Fairfax, Va., on September 6, 1973.

52. Hysom, pp. 125, 169, 180.

53. *Code of the County of Fairfax, Virginia*, vol. II, chap. 6, "The Zoning Ordinance," 1954, pp. 20, 23.

54. Hysom, pp. 144-5.

55. Ibid., p. 56.

56. *The Citizen's Handbook and Annual Report*, p. 54.

57. Office of the Chairman of the Board, "Fairfax County Boards, Authorities, Commissions, etc., Appointed by the Board of Supervisors." (Fairfax County, November 1, 1973).

58. Ibid.

59. Ibid.

60. Interview with Donald C. Stevens, attorney, Hazel, Beckhorn, & Hanes, and former county attorney, Fairfax County, in the city of Fairfax, Va., on September 5, 1973.

61. Ibid.

62. Ibid.

63. *Five Year Countywide Development Program*, p. xiii.

64. *Washington Post*, July 10, 1973.

65. *Washington Post*, Jan. 9, 1973.

66. Interview with Mr. Stevens.

67. Interview with Richard P. Bonar, planner, Gulf-Reston Corporation, and former planner, Fairfax County Division of Planning, in Reston, Va., on August 20, 1973.

68. *Washington Post*, Feb. 8, 1972.

69. *Five Year Countywide Development Program*, p. 8.

70. Hysom, pp. 224, 268.

71. *Five Year Countywide Development Program*, vol. II, pp. xxii, xxiii.

72. Interview with Mr. Stevens.

73. Inspections Division, Department of County Development, Fairfax County, 1973.

74. International City Managers' Association, *Management Information Service Report*, vol. 6, no. 5, May 1974, p. 8.

75. Office of Research and Statistics, Fairfax County, 1974.

76. "Staff Analysis of Effects of Emergency Interim Development Control Ordinance and Planning Commission Recommendation Regarding the Ordinance," (Fairfax County, 1974), p. 24.

77. Department of Assessments, Fairfax County, 1973.

78. Interview with Mr. Croom.

79. Inspections Division, Department of County Development, Fairfax County, 1972.

80. "Staff Analysis of Effects," pp. 24, 26.

81. Philip H. Davidson and B. Gayle Ennis, *Economic Review* (Washington: Federal Reserve Board, January 1974) in "Staff Analysis of Effects," p. 17.

82. "Staff Analysis of Effects," p. 16.

83. Interview with Mr. Stevens.

84. Task Force on Comprehensive Planning and Land Use Control, *Proposal for Implementing an Improved Planning and Land Use Control System in Fairfax County*, June 11, 1973, pp. 12-15.

85. *Code of Virginia*, chap. 15, Title 15.1-446.

86. Task Force on Comprehensive Planning and Land Use Control, p. 8.

87. Jim Reid, "Status Report No. 1 on the Planning and Land Use System (PLUS) Program" (Fairfax County, September 12, 1973), p. 6.

88. Ibid., p. 6.

89. Ibid., pp. 10-24.

90. Ibid., p. 6.

91. Task Force on Comprehensive Planning and Land Use Control, pp. 130-32.

92. Ibid., p. 120.

93. Reid, "Status Report No. 1," p. 8.

94. *Washington Star-News*, Feb. 14, 1974.

95. Jim Reid, "Establishment of Task Forces to Complete Analysis of Existing Conditions and Trend Analysis, Development of Policies and Objectives Statements, and Establishment of Priorities for Analysis" (Fairfax County, November 27, 1973).

96. Jim Reid, "Status Report No. 2 on the Planning and Land Use System (PLUS) Program" (Fairfax County, November 30, 1973), p. 4.

97. Michael Feiler, *Zoning Digest* vol. 24 (1972) p. 193.

98. Task Force on Comprehensive Planning and Land Use Control, p. 11.

99. Ibid., p. 12.

100. Ibid., pp. 144-5.

101. Reid, "Status Report No. 1," p. 7.

102. Ibid., p. 13.

103. Reid, "Status Report No. 2," p. 1.

104. Northern Virginia Planning District Commission, *Northern Virginia Metro Station Impact Study, Phase 1: Inventory Analysis*, April 1973, pp. 103-4.

105. *Washington Post*, Feb. 23, 1974.

106. Ibid., Dec. 13, 1973.

107. Reid, "Status Report No. 1," pp. 6-7.

108. Ibid., p. 3.

109. Task Force on Comprehensive Planning and Land Use Control, p. 8.

110. Reid, "Status Report No. 1," pp. 16 and 21.

111. Ibid., p. 17.

112. Ibid., p. 19.

113. Ibid., p. 24.

114. Interview with Arthur S. Drea, Jr., attorney, Meatyard and Carlin, and

former zoning hearing examiner, Montgomery County, Md., in Bethesda, Md., on August 22, 1973.

115. *Washington Post*, May 11, 1973.

116. Jim Reid, "Status Report No. 5 on the Planning and Land Use System (PLUS) Program: March 1-31" (Fairfax County, April 5, 1974) p. 3.

117. *Code of Virginia*, chap. 15, Title 15.1-437.

118. Reid, "Status Report No. 5," p. 3.

Bibliography

Bibliography

1960 Annual Report, Fairfax County, 1961.

1962 Annual Report, Fairfax County, 1963.

1966 Annual Report, Fairfax County, 1967.

1967 Annual Report, Fairfax County, 1968.

1968 Annual Report, Fairfax County, 1969.

1969 Annual Report, Fairfax County, 1970.

The Citizen's Handbook and Annual Report, FY 72, Fairfax County, January 1973.

Code of the County of Fairfax, Virginia, vol. II, chap. 6, "The Zoning Ordinance," 1954.

Code of Virginia, chap. 11, Title 14.1-46, 15.1-493, 494; chap. 15, Title 15.1-437, 446, 765, 766, 779.

Cresap, McCormick and Paget. "Fairfax County Management Audit of the County Government Organization and Operation: Preliminary Recommendations," 1968.

Davidson, Philip H. and B. Gayle Ennis. *Economic Review*. Washington, D.C.: Federal Reserve Board, January 1974, in "Staff Analysis of Effects of Emergency Interim Development Control Ordinance and Planning Commission Recommendation Regarding the Ordinance." Fairfax County, 1974.

Feiler, Michael. *Zoning Digest*. vol. 24, 1972.

Five Year Countywide Development Program: Presentation of Alternatives. vols. I and II Fairfax County, August 7, 1972.

Hysom, John L., Jr. "An Evaluation of the Effects of the Planning and Zoning Criteria Used for Allocating Land for Residential Purposes in Fairfax County, Virginia." Doctoral dissertation, The American University, second draft, May 15, 1973.

International City Managers' Association. *Management Information Service Report*. vol. 6, no. 5, May 1974.

Northern Virginia Planning District Commission. *Northern Virginia Metro Impact Study. Phase 1: Inventory Analysis*. April 1973, pp. 87-157.

Office of the Chairman of the Board. "Fairfax County Boards, Authorities, Commissions, etc., Appointed by the Board of Supervisors." Fairfax County, November 1, 1973.

Office of Research and Statistics. "Techniques for Improving Board Procedures with Special Attention to Administrative Procedures." Fairfax County, September 1973.

Population Reference Bureau. "Suburban Growth: A Case Study," *Population Bulletin*, vol. 28, no. 1. Washington, D.C., 1972.

"Proposed Department of County Development." Fairfax County, 1968.

Reid, Jim. "Establishment of Task Forces to Complete Analysis of Existing

Conditions and Trend Analysis, Development of Policies and Objectives Statements, and Establishment of Priorities for Analysis." Fairfax County, November 27, 1973.

Reid, Jim. "Status Report No. 1 on the Planning and Land Use System (PLUS) Program." Fairfax County, September 12, 1973.

_____. "Status Report No. 2 on the Planning and Land Use System (PLUS) Program." Fairfax County, November 30, 1973.

_____. "Status Report No. 3 on the Planning and Land Use System (PLUS) Program, December 3, 1973-January 31, 1974." Fairfax County, February 7, 1974.

_____. "Status Report No. 5 on the Planning and Land Use System, March 1-31, 1974." Fairfax County, April 5, 1974.

"Staff Analysis of Effects of Emergency Interim Development Control Ordinance and Planning Commission Recommendation Regarding the Ordinance." Fairfax County, 1974.

Task Force on Comprehensive Planning and Land Use Control. *Proposal for Implementing an Improved Planning and Land Use System in Fairfax County.* Fairfax County, June 11, 1973.

Traffic and Safety Division, Virginia Department of Highways. *Average Daily Traffic Volumes on Interstate, Arterial, and Primary Routes, 1962-3.* Richmond, 1963.

_____. *Average Daily Traffic Volumes on Interstate, Arterial, and Primary Routes, 1972.* Richmond, 1973.

U.S. Bureau of the Census. *Census of Housing 1960.* Virginia, HC(1). Washington: U.S. Government Printing Office.

_____. *Census of Housing 1970.* Virginia, HC(1). Washington: U.S. Government Printing Office.

_____. *Census of Population 1950.* Virginia, PC(1)-B. Washington: U.S. Government Printing Office.

_____. *Census of Population 1960.* Virginia, PC(1)-48B, C, D. Washington: U.S. Government Printing Office.

_____. *Census of Population 1970.* Virginia, PC(1)-48B and C. Washington: U.S. Government Printing Office.

_____. *Census of Population and Housing 1970.* Washington, D.C.-Md.-Va. SMSA, PHC(1)-226. Washington: U.S. Government Printing Office.

Washington Post. Feb. 8, 1972; Jan. 9, 1973; May 11, 1973; July 10, 1973; Dec. 13, 1973; Feb. 23, 1974.

Washington Star-News, Feb. 14, 1974.

About the Author

Terry Spielman Peters is a land use planner with the Arlington County (Virginia) Division of Planning. She received the B.A. in Public Affairs from the University of Chicago and the M.A. in Urban Affairs from Virginia Polytechnic Institute and State University. Previously, Ms. Peters performed housing research at the Washington Center for Metropolitan Studies.